Party Planning and Entertainment

BY THE SAME AUTHOR
Conjuring as a Craft

Party Planning
and Entertainment

IAN ADAIR

Line drawings by the author
Photographs by A. C. Littlejohns
and the author

DAVID & CHARLES : NEWTON ABBOT

0 7153 5268 7

Set in 11 on 13pt Times Roman
and printed in Great Britain
by Bristol Typesetting Company Limited Bristol
for David & Charles (Publishers) Limited
South Devon House   Newton Abbot   Devon

To my Mother

ISABEL ADAIR

Contents

List of Illustrations

1

Planning the Party

THE secret of success in almost anything one under-takes is *planning*, whether it is building a house or organising a party. Just as a well-built house must stand on sound foundations, so your party must be thoroughly well planned from the initial idea right through to its triumphal conclusion.

'Planning' and 'presentation' go together in party-giving and it is often small but clever touches in the manner in which a party is staged which lift it up above the ordinary run and make it a really memorable occasion. The various ways in which this can be achieved is the principal theme of this book, which covers most aspects of party planning with the exception of catering, a subject on which a number of admirable books have already been written. Important though food and drinks are, however, your guests will also want to be entertained, to be kept amused and happy, and it is here, it is hoped, that this book will be of practical assistance.

Parties fall into several different categories with the very young at one end of the scale, adults at the other, and a variety of ages and special occasions in between.

Planning successful parties for children calls for experience and certain qualities in the planner. One must be fond of children, know the type of entertainment they like best and have the ability to control them kindly but firmly. As children can soon get bored and restless, it is advisable to plan every detail of their party and there is advice later on how best to get them to know one another, how to keep them well-behaved during the entertainment, the best methods of distributing gifts and other such aids to organisation.

Adults' parties can equally be made or ruined by good forward planning, or the lack of it. Even if the main programme is an aperitif, dinner and a few drinks later in the evening, there could still be awkward intervals before the meal and afterwards which a little thought would have avoided. One or two intelligent games, impromptu diversions or interesting amusements can fill such gaps, and could well make the party a memorable one.

Even when dining out with friends in a restaurant a little forward planning, such as arranging a presentation of flowers to a lady guest to mark some special occasion or for a favourite tune to be played if there is music, does not come amiss and could ensure the success of the evening.

To turn now to the detail of party planning, let us start with a look at what lies behind the successful organisation of various kinds of parties for children.

CHILDREN'S PARTIES

We will assume that you are a parent and are perhaps organising a birthday party for your child. It is going to be your child's day, a special event just for him or her. First, you will have to decide who is to be invited, the games to be played, a possible entertainment spot, and details of the birthday tea, complete with extras such as sweets, decorations and surprises.

You will find out who your child would like to invite, and you will no doubt also take into account the parties to which your child has been invited, for this is an obvious opportunity to return such hospitality.

A most important point is to make sure that you do not invite more children than you can cope with, for there is nothing worse than having a 'packed house' which you cannot control. Consider, then, both the size of your home and your purse and limit your party guests to the number you are confident can be comfortably accommodated and generously fed. In other words, let 'quality rather than quantity' be your party maxim and don't hope to rely on the excuse that your party got out of control because too many children turned up.

When you have finally decided who is to be invited, formal invitations should be sent out. These are your first contacts with your potential guests and should be made as attractive as possible, so that they will wish to come. A variety of suitable cards are available from good stationers and are rather more impressive than hand-written notes. Remember that the cards should state the name of the person being invited, the date of the event, whose party it is, where it is to take place, the time it will start *and the time it will end,* all important points which are too often forgotten. There should be a request to the invited guests to state whether they can attend. A simple answer of 'Yes or No' is all that is required.

The invitations should be posted three weeks before the event is due to take place, no later and, in my opinion, no earlier. If longer notice is given, the event is apt to seem too distant and may be forgotten, and if presented too close to the actual date, the notice may be insufficient and other arrangements may already have been made by those invited.

You will, of course, have arranged for your party to start at a reasonable time, depending upon the age of the children. Young children of three, four and five years of age should not be expected to stay up late, so that an afternoon party is ideal for such an age bracket, the party commencing at 3.0 p.m. and ending about 5.30. A good tip, in this case, is to announce that your party will end at 5.15, as some parents will surely turn up late to collect their children and this will give you a little leeway. Those who do arrive before the end of the party can join in the fun and perhaps appreciate what a clever host or hostess you are!

Far too many children's parties are spoilt by being allowed to go on for too long. Children, specially at an early age, soon get tired when engaged in activities to which they are not normally accustomed. Far better than sending your young guests home exhausted, to see them off excitedly chattering about the wonderful party they have had.

Times have now been fixed, the answers to your invitations have been received and the number of guests you can expect is known to you. You are part-way there. Cancellations may later occur and often do, but your general plan should remain unaltered and based on the original number of acceptances.

Birthday or party teas should, of course, be prepared in advance, preferably in a different room from that in which the games and entertainments are to take place. This gives the organiser a chance to prepare and clear up without interruption while the fun and games are in full swing elsewhere.

Before the tea the children are fresh, and this is the ideal time for introducing a few lively games of the type one knows will be acceptable to all children. Many kinds of games will be described later but the best ones for opening a party are those which give the children an opportunity to mix and meet the others present. As adults, we know how embarrassing it can be to attend a dinner or party where one is not acquainted with the majority of people present. Children are naturally good mixers and do not have all the inhibitions of their parents but, even so, a few rollicking games can start everything off on a friendly and jolly note. Everyone should be given an opportunity of joining in the fun. No one should feel left out.

Later in this book, in addition to the games already mentioned, the reader will be offered a number of suggestions for suitable forms of entertainment. It is, of course, possible to obtain the services of a professional entertainer, such as a magician (certainly the best type of entertainer for a child's party) or a puppeteer to provide an interlude of make-believe amongst the organised games. However, the services of an entertainer may not always be available and in some cases fees can be quite high. This book will offer alternatives, enabling you to provide your own entertainment and so perhaps bring extra credit to yourself. Origami (paper folding) and conjuring, for example, can prove most successful forms of party entertainment and we shall return to these later.

Let us now assume you have given your guests a thoroughly enjoyable party, consisting of a few lively games to begin with, a pleasant tea, perhaps a quiz session, several stunts, puzzles and entertainment, and that you are now getting ready to close the proceedings. One final game can be an excellent way of rounding off a well-balanced and properly organised party, one which, thanks to the planning behind it, has had plenty of audience participation.

As the children's ages range in different groups, so must

the pattern of your parties vary. Games suitable for three-year-old children are 'babyish' to those of nine, ten or twelve years old, and my selections of games have been designed to cater for children of all ages. As a parent, you will not need to be told of the likely attitude of an older child asked to play games designed for younger children!

FACTORY PARTIES FOR CHILDREN

You have been put in charge of the factory children's party, perhaps the Christmas one. Some large factories are in the happy position of being able to employ outside caterers who will also provide the entertainments and an experienced games-master to control the children. But services like these are expensive and many smaller firms have to work to a rather tight budget. Nevertheless, with good organisation their party can be just as well planned and every bit as successful as the others; in fact, in many cases they can be very much more enjoyable.

Here are some important steps towards making such a party a success.

At a large factory party many of the children are meeting for the first time. They therefore tend to congregate in groups, and these should be broken up as much as possible in the interests of the party as a whole. With this in mind all the children should be encouraged to participate in all the games and activities with the others. If the party is for a mixed-age group, it is even more difficult to plan the games and these have then to be carefully chosen so that everyone attending can take part and enjoy them.

Invitation cards should be properly printed or nicely duplicated and should include the time, place and date of the event. These should be sent to all employees without exception who have children. It is important that the

Page 17: Two in One Go. (*top left*) Coins balanced on edge of tumbler; (*top right*) thumb and forefinger press on top; (*bottom left*) coins slide down side of tumbler; (*bottom right*) coins held between thumb and finger

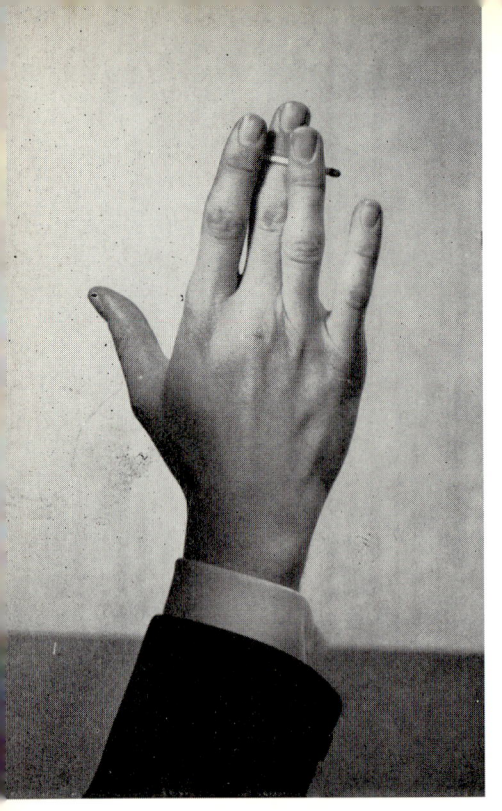

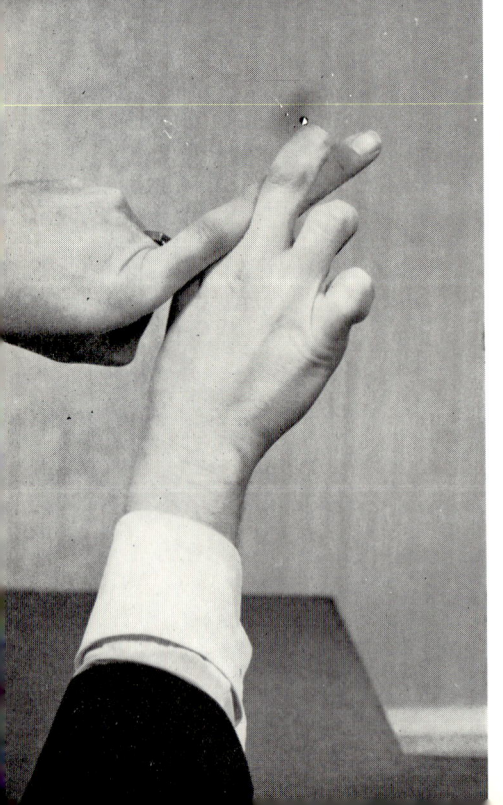

Page 18 : (*top left*) Snap a Match, the correct position; (*top right*) Crazy Peg, balancing peg with strap; (*below*) making a long finger

organisers should know the approximate number of children who will be coming and it is a good idea to arrange for a perforated counterfoil at one side of the invitation card, on which the parent can fill in the child's name and address in acceptance of the invitation, tear it off and return it to the main office at the factory. Alternatively, arrangements can be made for the slips to be collected by a certain date. In either case, allowance should be made for late acceptances by parents who have overlooked the return date or temporarily mislaid their invitation cards. So if, for example, you have had acceptances for a total of eighty children, you would be wise to cater for approximately one hundred.

The party tea must be organised in a separate room apart from where the games are to take place and the games themselves should all be team games. After tea, an entertainment of some sort should be provided which will give the children an opportunity to settle down and the organisers a chance to clear the tables before their services are again required later during the party.

Make sure that all the children have an opportunity of going to the toilets after tea, before any organised entertainment starts. There is nothing worse for the entertainer than to have a long trek of children going to and from the lavatories throughout his performance. Young children may need some help and there should be a male to look after the boys and a female assistant for the girls. And if, as is often the case, a child gets over-excited or feels strange among so many others and bursts into tears, a woman helper should be available to deal with the situation, and can usually be relied upon to solve the child's problem.

Another point to watch: if, for lack of space, the entertainment is being given in the same room as that in which the tea was served, make sure that your helpers clear up *quietly.* Noise can be a serious distraction for the entertainer and for the children who are trying to watch or listen to him.

For ease of reference, this book has been sectionalised as much as possible, and party stunts and various forms of entertainment from fortune-telling and conjuring to Origami should enable you to select without difficulty those best suited to your particular requirements. The various stunts can be selected and slotted into your programme, as necessary. But above all, make sure that the whole programme is properly planned and that you know exactly what you are going to do, and when you are going to do it.

Still dealing with the factory children's party, it may be decided that each child is to be presented with a gift. If so, this should be done at the end of the party, forming the perfect climax to it, otherwise there will be gift wrappings and toys all over the place, causing distraction and possible hazards throughout the rest of the programme.

There are several better ways of distributing gifts than just 'handing out packets' and the following method has been tried and tested most successfully.

Providing the gifts inside are suitable for either boys or girls, each gift is wrapped and on a plain gummed label attached to it is written part of an obvious 'double'. For example, 'Jack' is written on one parcel, 'Salt' on another, and so on. Another set of labels carry the words which pair to make the 'double', for example 'Jill' (Jack and Jill), 'Pepper' (Salt and Pepper) are placed inside a drum or container and mixed up, and each child in turn is invited to pick out a label from it. When they shout out their word, completing the double, they take away their gift.

The gifts are given on the spot, one at a time, and not all together at the end, which would result in one big scramble. By this method you have not only presented the gifts in an orderly manner but you have also created another game which is both entertaining and exciting.

Here are some suggestions for the doubles.

Hot and *cold*; rain and *sun*; heavy and *light*; red, white and *blue*; fish and *chips*; Tom, Dick and *Harry*; soldier, sailor, tinker, *tailor*; rich and *poor*; young and *old*; bright and *dull*; fast and *slow*; good and *bad*; right and *wrong*; black and *white*; thin and *fat*; loose and *tight*; salt and *pepper*; pen and *paper*; table and *chair*; cup and *saucer*; bow and *arrow*.

Many other such doubles will come to mind, and there should be no difficulty in compiling as long a list as is required.

A more conventional method of distributing the gifts is to have each child's name written upon the parcel, or on a tag or label attached to it. Santa Claus, if it is a Christmas party, can then distribute the gifts, or one of the organisers can call out each name loudly and clearly, waiting until the gift has been claimed before he deals with the next package.

So the factory party is over. Everyone has had a good time, and during the fun the helpers have been clearing away the tea tables and have now finished their work. The organisers should have made clear on the invitation card the time when the child was to be collected, and should again have allowed themselves a little leeway. In which case, during the presentation of the gifts or the final games, the parents will be arriving at intervals ready to take their children home. Long bench seats should be available for them to sit on for the short time they may have to wait, and these should be set around the hall where they will not hamper the final games or the distribution of presents.

CHURCH, SUNDAY-SCHOOL AND PRIMARY PARTIES

This book would not be complete without reference to parties organised by religious groups, for many thousands are given by them each year. Sunday-school Christmas parties, primary parties for the younger children, boy scout and girl guide parties are but a few that come to mind. Such parties are often held in the church hall, and as the funds usually come from charity or from church collections and are likely to be limited, then any games, entertainment or catering will have to be planned with the minimum of expense.

Fortunately, such organisations can almost always rely upon any amount of voluntary help. Sunday-school teachers will give up their time and often provide some of the necessary funds to ensure that the children have a good time. Local scout groups, if approached, may gladly provide the entertainment, while the girl guides may be equally ready to help with the catering, and even perhaps to display their skill as cake-makers.

ORGANISING THE SUNDAY-SCHOOL PARTY

Let us assume that this is a regular seasonal event, perhaps taking place at Christmas, for all children who attend the classes. To organise such a party there should first be a meeting, attended by the minister of the church, the teachers and other members of the congregation willing to help, at which it should be decided when the party is to take place, the time, and the venue. Normally the party takes place in the church hall, which gives the organisers an advantage over other groups, for they will know when it is available. When these points have been agreed upon, the meeting can then get down to planning the general pattern of the party.

So far as food is concerned, a ' sandwich ' buffet is often the answer for such an occasion as this. It is comparatively easy to arrange and is also the most economical of all party teas. Sandwiches—if the fillings are sufficiently varied—plus cakes and soft drinks, usually delight young guests, who never seem to ask for anything else, nor to expect it.

The quantity to be provided is best based on a ratio of four sandwiches per child, plus two cakes. Some children will have one, some two, and some five or six, but by averaging *four* sandwiches to a child, the party organiser will find that he is providing an adequate amount for all.

Children nowadays are sophisticated enough to want something a little out of the ordinary, so make your sandwiches small and varied. Double-decker sandwiches are far more interesting than single ones and should be cut into slim fingers; open sandwiches, too, are very popular. Items like cheese with chopped nuts, decorated with chopped cherries, small cocktail sausages on sticks, and lumps of pineapple and cheese on sticks, are greeted with delight. It is a good idea to get some large, firm cabbages, cut them in half and impale the sticks all over them so they rather resemble decorated porcupines on the table.

Be sure to cut all the crust off the bread, using a sharp knife, and remember that not all sandwich fillings have to be savoury ones. Especially delicious sweet ones are very easily and economically prepared. One good method is to make two basic white sauces, a sweet one and a savoury one, and to use these for moistening and enhancing the flavour of the various sandwich fillings.

The consumption of soft drinks does not need to be so carefully calculated as they will keep and any unwanted bottles can be used on another occasion. Alternatively, an

23

arrangement can often be made with a local mineral-water company or supplier to provide an ample supply and to take back any bottles that were not required.

The party tea should be laid upon trestle tables, and if possible on disposable paper tablecloths. Again, the tea should be kept separate from the games and entertainment, which, ideally, should take place in a different part of the hall.

No invitation cards are needed for such a party but, some three weeks before the event, teachers at their usual Sunday meeting should announce the party and ask which of the children would like to attend. Their names should be entered in a ledger or notebook, so that the total number attending will be known, and the children should be reminded to be sure to tell their parents about the party. It might even be advisable for each child to take home a card upon which is written the time, day and explanation of the event, so that the parents will know what arrangements to make.

As most Sunday-schools have several teachers attending each meeting, each with their own class, it is essential to have one main organiser for the party, who then delegates various responsibilities to the others. If there are too many people dealing with similar matters there is liable to be misunderstandings, confusion and wasted effort. Far better that each teacher should be told exactly what to do, and when to do it, so that all have their own individual tasks.

As the function is non-profit-making and under church auspices, the organisers may find it possible to enlist the free services of an entertainer, especially if such a one is a member of their congregation. Many entertainers who normally receive fees for their performances are often willing to give their services free to such worthwhile causes. Some may insist on payment, but will then make a donation to the church corresponding to the amount of the fee they have charged. This may seem rather peculiar, but professional etiquette may be involved, and by this procedure the performer can, in effect, provide both free entertainment and make a donation to the church.

Alternatively, it should not be too difficult to find a sponsor or sponsors amongst the congregation who would be willing to defray the entertainer's fee. After all, if he is a professional he can hardly be expected to work for nothing, any more than the baker and the caterer could be expected to give away their wares. Such fees are usually quite reasonable, and if he is good, a professional entertainer will give a special cachet to a party and so help to make it an outstanding one.

Games which would be suitable for such an occasion are discussed later and, because the children concerned all meet each other regularly, a Sunday-school party can perhaps be regarded as the most sociable of all parties and the least difficult to organise. There is no 'ice to break', everybody is friends, and the party gets off to a good start.

CHILDREN'S PARTY GIFTS

At birthday parties, gifts are usually presented by the guests to the birthday child, unless of course you state specifically on your invitation card 'No birthday gifts, please'. This is quite a nice idea, as not all parents wish their guests to bear this obligatory expense.

The best procedure when receiving presents is for the child to be told to thank each guest for their gift and for these then to be taken into a separate room and left there. Several gifts may be presented at one time, or in rotation, and if all are put to one side there will be no risk of upsets

25

over possible duplication of items. In the course of the party, the birthday child may be allowed to go to the room on his or her own and unwrap the parcels and, towards the end of the party, should thank the guests again for their presents, as they leave.

An alternative is for the gifts to be left unopened until the party is over. Then, when all the guests have gone, the child can open them at leisure, with time to examine and enjoy each individual present.

ADULT PARTIES

Adult parties can, perhaps, be generally classified as Christmas and New Year celebrations, anniversary parties (which can cover a multitude of things) birthdays (including 21st birthdays), house warmings, going-away parties, cocktail parties, small private home parties, office and factory parties, out-of-door parties, and parties given at a restaurant or catering hall.

As most of these parties are held in the home, the entertainment can fairly easily be provided. The main requirements will be a good supply of gramophone records, a small area in which to dance, a couple of packs of cards, plus some of the interesting and quite exciting proprietary games which are available, and perhaps a few 'stunts' and ideas culled from this book.

If it is to be a birthday or anniversary party, names should be carefully listed to make sure that no one of importance has been left out. When the number of guests has been decided upon, each should be sent an invitation card three weeks before the party is due to take place. The time, date and place at which the party is to be held should be clearly stated. For instance:

PLANNING THE PARTY

MR and MRS J. SMITH
request the pleasure of your
company on the occasion of their
Silver Wedding anniversary
at their residence, 11 High Street, Manchester
7.0 for 7.30 pm, Saturday, 4 December 1971
RSVP

When the number of acceptances is known, you make your plans accordingly. Stunts, quizzes, intelligence games, conjuring entertainment and Origami can be used to good effect at such a party, whereas if no particular activities have been planned there can be a somewhat strained atmosphere, with people striving, not always with any noticeable success, to keep up the flow of conversation. A well-timed interlude of entertainment not only helps to break the ice and enliven the proceedings, but also provides interesting 'talking points' and shows your guests that you have gone to some trouble to keep them entertained.

Here are a few small but nonetheless important points to remember:

In winter, make sure the room is well heated before your guests arrive.

Upon their arrival, take your guests' coats, hats and handbags, see that they are kept together, and put them in a separate room ready for collection at the end of the party.

Be ready to receive your guests at the commencement of the party. Listen for the door-bell!

Offer your guests a chair and introduce them to all your other friends, if they do not already know them.

Offer your guests a drink but make it *clear* what you have to offer. Never make the mistake of saying 'What will you have?' A small bar in one corner of your room, perhaps converted from a large table or sideboard and covered with a tablecloth, can be used to display the drinks and show your guests exactly what you have to offer.

Do not encourage guests to help themselves—or supplies may run out sooner than you had allowed for.

Whenever a bottle becomes empty, remove it so that you will not disappoint a guest if he requires a refill later on.

Make sure you have ice, cocktail sticks, cherries, a lemon or two, plain water and soda water, bitter lemon, orange, lime, Coca-Cola, and the other accessories which go with most drinks.

Assorted nuts, olives, small cocktail onions, cocktail biscuits and potato crisps, and a small canapés such as cream cheese or meat paté on small crisp biscuits, are always popular when served with the aperitif.

These can be served in dishes divided into six or seven sections or placed in a series of separate small dishes strategically distributed about the room so that guests may readily help themselves.

'POP' PARTIES

A 'pop music party' is ideal for teenagers, who will have grown out of games designed for children, but will no doubt, like their friends, be 'pop' record enthusiasts. Such a party can easily be arranged and without heavy expense.

No invitation cards are required, as the teenage host will usually prefer personally to invite friends along. It also provides an excellent opportunity for inviting particular boy or girl friends, or that special person they have always wanted to know.

An adult, preferably the mother of the teenager, should be present if the young guests are sixteen years of age or

under, to keep the party under control without unduly re-
stricting the guests' freedom. The parent can also help in
organising the party, preparing and serving the food, and
generally making sure that everything runs smoothly.

The room should be furnished with comfortable chairs or,
as many teenagers prefer, with cushions scattered on the
floor. The record-player is obviously the central attraction,
and as it is usual for other guests to bring along their
personal records, these should be marked, perhaps with the
owner's initials on the labels, so that no confusion arises
at the end of the party.

A buffet meal, at which guests can serve themselves, is
much the best arrangement for such a party, and also allows
all preparations to be made in advance. Remember, too,
that teenagers like the more savoury and sophisticated foods
for their entertaining.

Such a party, commencing at 7.0 pm and ending about
10.30, should provide teenagers with ample time in which
to enjoy a very pleasant and successful 'pop party'.

FILM SHOW PARTIES

Film entertainments are always popular with guests, both
young and old, and here again advance planning is all-
important. A suitable atmosphere, adequate and comfortable seating arrangements and the right choice of films for
your audience are but three points requiring careful con-
sideration. Another is the length of the film show; one hour
is about right for most parties, perhaps a little less if the
entertainment is for children.

Films of 8mm are frequently used for small parties but
the standard 16mm ones are more suitable for larger gather-
ings. Silent films are no longer attractive to audiences accustomed to television, and colour films, which cost little more

29

to hire, are much to be preferred to black-and-white versions.

For children's parties, the best age group has been found to be the six-year-olds and over; younger children quickly become restless and can spoil the show for others. Children at a party like the fantasy type of film rather than an educational one. They dislike travel films and positively hate movies which involve conversations between several persons, becoming confused by too many voices talking at the same time. Cartoons are extremely popular and are available in a wide range, with excellent sound accompaniment. In presenting such a show, films should be spliced carefully together so that each cartoon blends smoothly into the next and there is no distraction or break in the 'magic' while spools are being changed. Films are usually projected over the children's heads, and in a drawing-room showing the children can be happily seated on the floor.

For the host who already has his own projector and screen, and knows how to use them, a film show presents no difficulties and if he has no suitable films of his own for a particular party there is a wide selection available for hire from the various film agencies.

If he does not have a projector but still wants to present the show himself, all the necessary equipment can be hired at no great expense, but unless he is confident of his ability to operate it successfully he would probably be better-advised to employ one of the mobile professional film units which specialise in private showings. The cost will be not much greater than hiring the equipment, and it is all too easy for the unskilled operator to damage film while it is going through the projector. And as a damaged colour film could cost as much as £400 to replace, and the risk is virtually uninsurable, the extra cost of engaging a qualified operator may be considered well worth while.

These mobile film units, which are becoming increasingly

popular in Britain, and indeed throughout the world, are professional groups who have made a special study of party entertainment. They provide all the necessary equipment, offer a wide choice of 16mm films—both monochrome and colour—with full sound effects, and are equally available for a small house party or a large factory or office gathering. Their fees range from £7.05 upwards, with an extra charge for functions beyond a radius of ten miles from their operating centre, and booking has generally to be made well in advance to enable them to obtain the particular type of film you may want for your entertainment. Many of the films used are made by the Children's Film Foundation on behalf of the large film companies and include good stories, providing excitement, laughter and suspense. The extra cost of these special films, which include such ever-popular favourites as Walt Disney's 'Snow White and the Seven Dwarfs' and 'Bambi', would bring the total fee for a birthday party film show up to £10 to £14.

Incidentally, it is not generally known that most feature films shown in cinemas can be obtained for private showing nine months after their general release. They can be shown at home without restriction and at a reasonable cost, but if presented in halls, clubs or at factory parties, cinema industry regulations stipulate that the venue must be *at least* two miles distant from the nearest public cinema. For such occasions the cost of hiring a feature film will depend upon the seating capacity of the hall or room, not upon the number of admissions.

If you decide to engage a professional mobile unit to present your film show, the questions to ask are: (i) Is the film 16mm sound? (ii) Are the films in colour? (iii) How long will the show last? (iv) Is it non-stop for the period stated? and (v) Is the fee inclusive?

Make sure, too, that you let the unit know the type of

audience for whom the show is intended, and if they are to be children, whether they will be boys or girls, or both, and their average age group. And if you are booking a particular film unit on the recommendation of a friend or neighbour, do not forget to mention this to the unit as parties have sometimes been spoilt by children being shown the same films that they saw at a near-by party only a few weeks earlier.

The major film companies—Rank, United Artists, Columbia Pictures, Paramount, M.G.M. and 20th Century Fox—can usually recommend a reliable 16mm mobile film unit in your area, or they may be traced through the yellow pages of your telephone directory. A number of such organisations are also listed in the Appendix at the end of this book.

RECORDS AND COPYRIGHT RESTRICTIONS

Although records can be played at private parties and other small functions without infringement of copyright, this problem does arise when an entertainment is open to the public, or where the sale of tickets is involved.

The Copyright Act does not precisely define a 'public performance' but on the basis of a considerable body of precedent it may be broadly stated that a performance which does not form part of the domestic or home life of those participating is 'public' within the meaning of the Act. Thus, a private party in the sense of a wedding reception or anniversary, a birthday party or similar events to which the organiser invites only his relatives and friends, ie, members of the home circle, would be considered private and no licence would be required if records were played, irrespective of whether the party was held in a private residence or in a local hall hired for the purpose. On the other hand, where persons attend events as part of their outside or non-domestic life in pursuit of some common interest, performances given under those conditions would be public within the meaning of the Act, eg, club activities, works and office functions and such like.

Moreover, when copyright music is thus given a public performance by means of gramophone records, two copyrights are involved and consequently two licences are required. The first, the licence of the Performing Rights Society Limited, relates to the copyright in the musical works reproduced on records and is issued on behalf of the composers of the music. The second, the licence of Phonographic Performance Limited, relates to the entirely separate copyright which subsists in gramophone records as such, quite apart and distinct from the musical works reproduced thereon.

Phonographic Performance Limited is a company which was founded by the leading British manufacturers of gramophone records with the object of controlling the public use of their records and issuing licences for that purpose. In this connection, the term, 'records' includes any commercial tape recordings which may be issued by these manufacturers. All revenue derived from licence fees is distributed among the recording companies, recording artistes and musicians.

It should also be remembered that the unauthorised re-recording or copying by any means, including magnetic tapes, of records constitutes an infringement of copyright and renders those responsible liable to legal action.

2
Games for Small Parties

THE games described in this chapter are ones particularly suitable for presentation at small parties where the number of guests does not exceed twenty and where floor space is limited. The games should be planned and the necessary preparations made well in advance of the event and, once under way, the organiser should exercise tactful but firm control of the proceedings. Otherwise, arguments are liable to develop or mishaps may occur.

Prizes may be awarded, if desired, to the winners of games, but these should be more in the nature of token awards than expensive presents. An orange or an apple, a small packet of cigarettes, a bar of chocolate, a pencil or a memorandum pad would all be quite adequate for the occasion.

TREASURE TROVE

Here is an interesting game which can be the hit of your party.

Your guests are provided with sheets, upon which are

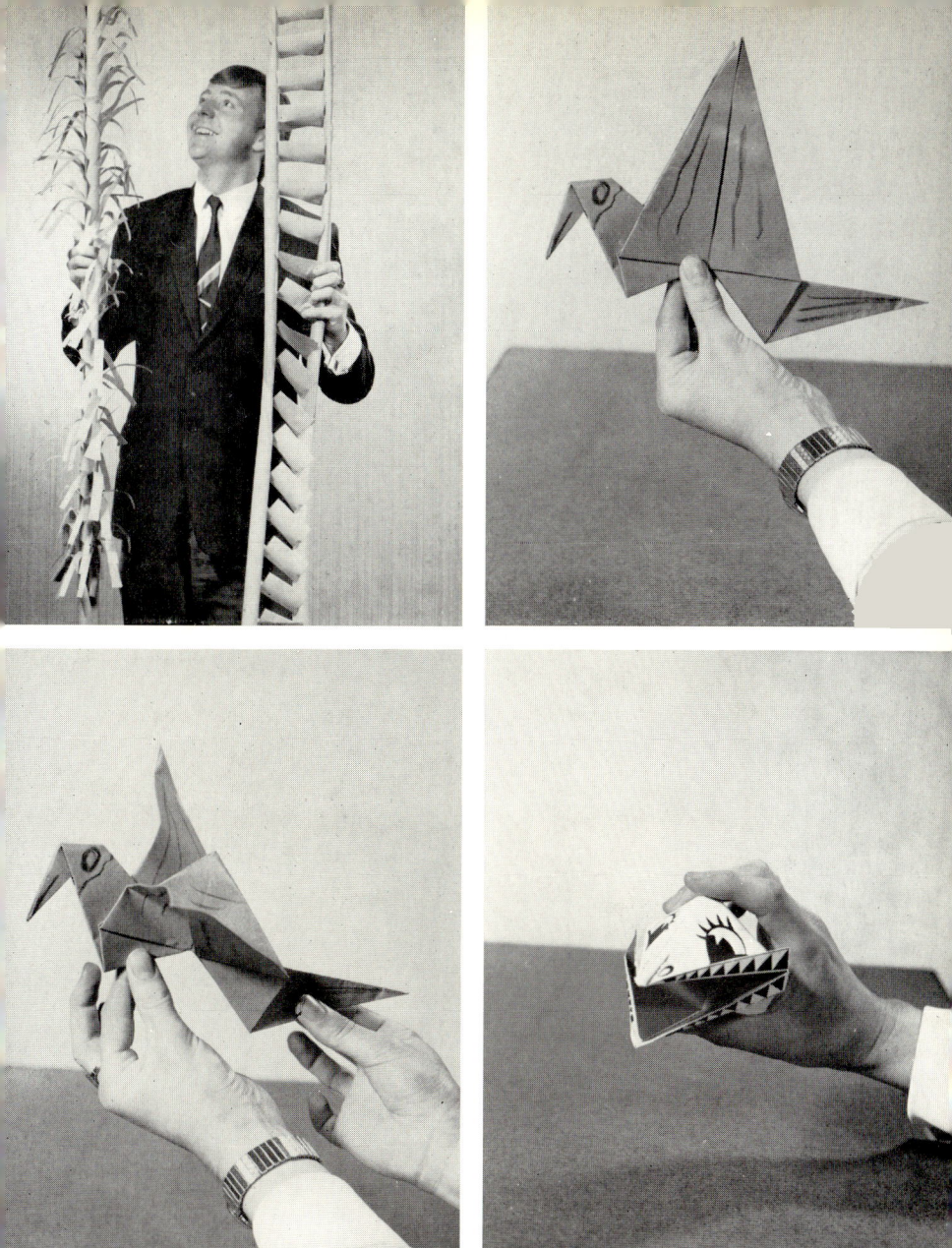

Page 35: (*top left*) Paper ladder and tree; (*top right*) the Flapping Bird model complete; (*bottom left*) wings flap when tail is pulled; (*bottom right*) Snake's mouth opens and closes under hand pressure

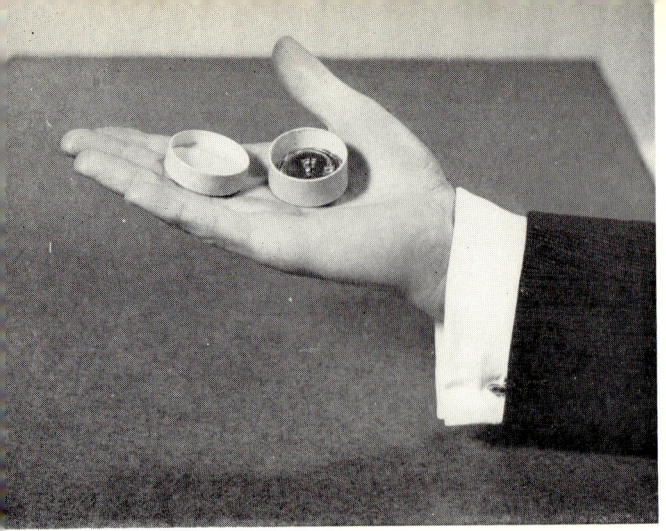

Page 36: How Time Flies:
(top) Box containing watch
rests on palm of hand;
(centre) the undercover
move: as lid is replaced,
box is allowed to pivot
over; (below) performer's
view: a quick glimpse at
the watch-face reveals the
chosen time

duplicated or written twenty or more items which you in-
tend using in this game. The main object of the game is for
the guests to find the hiding-place of each item listed. For
example, a postage stamp may be stuck to a picture on the
wall, a pipe can be hung on some ornament, a fountain pen
may be placed in a tumbler or a key on top of a radio, and
so on. In other words, an assortment of familiar objects
in unfamiliar places, but all distributed around the one
room.

Each guest is given a copy of the list and is asked to
discover and then write down the location of the various
articles. No article may be touched or moved during the
game and, of course, no guest should reveal the location
of an item to anyone else. More fun will be had if some of
the articles are harder to find than others; these could, for
example, be pinned to a curtain or wedged between books in
a bookcase, but don't make them *too* hard to find so that
your guests start lifting the carpets!

The guest who has listed the correct location of the greatest number of the hidden items is the winner. A time limit
for the game is advisable and should not exceed fifteen
minutes.

IT'S IN THE BAG

This is another ideal game to present at the small party,
especially when your guests are seated.

It is similar to the game just described but instead of the
guests being required to find a number of articles, they are
asked to identify by feel an assortment of articles which
have been mixed up inside a cloth bag. Ten items should be
used and these are placed in the bag, which is then firmly
secured at the top. The more unusual the articles and the
more peculiar their shapes the better. Sufficient space should

C

be allowed within the bag so that each article can be handled singly through the material and the bag is passed to each guest in turn. The one whose written list contains the greatest number of correct identifications, within the stated time limit, is the winner. Each player should be asked to write his or her name clearly on top of each slip before these are handed over to the host.

ROUND THE TABLE

Another somewhat similar game, this is ideal for about seven or eight guests. These sit around the table, with the host at the head, keeping their hands under the table and leaning slightly forward over the surface. From a covered shopping basket at his side containing a dozen different articles, the host extracts one item at a time which he passes to the guest on his right, who has to try to identify it by feel alone, and then pass it on to his next-door neighbour so that it proceeds, still under cover, round the table to finish up with the host who replaces it in the basket under the cloth. When all twelve articles have thus been circulated— and not until then—each guest is given a piece of paper and pencil and asked to write down the various items they have identified. The guest listing the most articles is the winner, and will certainly be someone who has a good memory.

ADVERTISEMENT GAME

This is an old game, but one which can bring a lot of fun to a party.

Cut out a dozen pictorial advertisements (some of them fairly familiar ones) which have appeared in recent news-papers or magazines. After the names of the advertisers have been cut off or erased, the advertisements are pasted or taped to a large sheet of cardboard, or onto a piece of plywood, and each is given a number, clearly marked with crayon or marker pen.

Guests who wish to join in the game are given sheets of paper on which the numbers 1 to 12 have been set out on separate lines and the one who first hands in a list on which all advertisers' names have been correctly identified is the outright winner. Again, there should be a time limit, and if no one succeeds in identifying all the advertisers, the one with the highest score is the winner. In the event of a tie, both players cut a pack of cards, the highest card determining the winner.

BLOW OUT THE CANDLE

Here each guest has the chance to blow out a candle—provided it can be located under a blindfold. The candle is placed upon the table and each guest, already blindfolded, is in turn spun around two or three times before being told to start to blow. The extraordinary antics that usually follow can be relied upon to keep any party highly amused. A time limit, say five minutes, is imposed, each guest is timed and the one who extinguishes the candle in the shortest time is the winner.

LISTEN CAREFULLY

A perfect party game, this, in which your guests can remain seated.

The host explains the rules and warns everyone that they must watch and listen very carefully if they hope to remain in the game.

. He then performs various antics, such as hand-clapping,

bobbing up and down, shaking his head and so on, each time saying 'Do this' or 'Do that'. The guests must imitate the antics only when the words 'Do this' are spoken. When 'Do that' is said, they must not copy the action. This often causes great confusion, and those guests who do imitate the host's actions when they should not, drop out of the game.

The surviving guest is the winner.

BEATING THE HANGMAN

A game suitable for six persons.

The guests stand in the middle of the floor with their index fingers outstretched, meeting everyone else's fingers in the centre. The host, representing the hangman, displays a small noose made of thin rope or cord which he drops over the fingers of the guests. When the word ' Drop ' is called, the guests must quickly withdraw their fingers. Any guest whose finger is caught in the noose has to retire, until only the winner remains.

CHINESE COOKING

An amusing game for two persons at a time.

Both guests are given a pair of chopsticks together with a bowl or saucer containing grains of rice. Each person should also have a tea-cup by his side. On the word of command 'Go!' both players start transferring the rice grains, singly and separately with the aid of the chopsticks, from the bowl to the tea-cup.

Both bowls should contain an equal amount of grains and the winner is the one who first succeeds in emptying his bowl.

SILHOUETTES

From local or national newspapers, cut out various photographs of well-known persons. With a marker pen, blacken their faces so they become silhouettes.

Guests are given paper and pencils and asked to write down the names of the celebrities. For best effect, the silhouettes should be mounted on a piece of heavy board.

NUMBER PUZZLE

A party game especially devised for this book.

Take several large cards and, making rough sketches with a bold marker pen, (your artwork does not need to be good) illustrate the following suggestions. Each drawing represents a number and guests have to identify the numbers to which the drawings correspond. Thus a drawing of a cat represents '9', the nine lives of a cat. Other drawings could depict a key (21); a magician pulling a rabbit from a hat—a hat trick (3); a policeman (999); a pear (2); Heinz Beans (57); a human foot (12) twelve inches; a man walking under a ladder (13); a bowl of sugar (16) sweet sixteen; a footballer scoring a goal, with a caption reading 'Good Score' (20) being a *score*.

Alternatively a board containing a montage of all the numbers used can be displayed, so that the guests may look at these and then try to match them with the drawings.

TELLING A STORY

Another amusing game which can be played with everyone seated. Chairs can be arranged around the room, or the guests can be seated at a large table.

The first guest writes a short story of some four sentences, and then whispers it to his neighbour. He, in turn, whispers what he remembers to his partner and so it goes on, until the story finally reaches the last guest. It is quite amazing, and most amusing, to hear the final story told aloud by the last guest, for by the time it has been whispered around the group it will have become wildly distorted. The original story, written down, can be referred to afterwards and compared with the final version.

LEGS

Not a game for every social gathering but one that goes down well at the right kind of party.

The ladies stand behind a screen or sheet so placed that only their legs are showing. The men are each given a piece of paper and a pencil and, after studying each pair of legs, have to write down the name of the lady to whom they think they belong. The ladies and positions should be numbered to avoid confusion, and this will also facilitate the filling-in of names to correspond with numbers on the paper.

YOUR CHARACTER REVEALED

The guests are given paper and pencils and each is asked to write down the names of six things which she or he dislikes. They then add their name at the top of the paper and hand it to their host.

The host reads aloud the contents of each paper, and the guests have to guess who is the owner of the various 'dislikes'. This can be a most amusing game and the means of some surprising revelations.

A PROPOSAL

The ideal party game for teenage functions.

A girl sits on the sofa whilst a boy kneels at her feet and proposes to her in his most eloquent manner. When each boy and girl have had their turn, the guests decide by vote who has made the best proposal. The girls, of course, have the choice of refusing or accepting the proposal, and the opportunity of making a gracious or even humorous reply.

YOUR LETTER

Each of the guests is presented with a piece of paper or card, at the head of which is boldly printed a letter of the alphabet. At the word 'Go!' each guest has to write down as many English proper nouns as he or she can think of beginning with that particular letter. Only one minute is allowed, after which a whistle is blown or a call given, and all sheets of paper are immediately handed over to the host. The winner is the one who has listed the greatest number of words using the given letter.

BLINDFOLD CARD GAME

This game is played by pairs seated either opposite one another at a table or at separate tables.

Several packs of playing-cards are spread all over the table. The men, on one side, are blindfolded, and the task of the ladies sitting opposite them is to help their respective partners. When the word is given, the blindfolded men try to pick up as many playing-cards as they can, their partners guiding them by verbal directions as to where the cards are to be found. The man must pick up only one card at a time, and the winners are, of course, the pair which manages to secure the most cards.

TAPE-RECORDER FUN

This is a game I devised some years ago for a special party, and it proved so successful that my guests have often introduced it since at their own parties.

As your guests arrive one by one or in groups, you invite them to record their voice on your tape-recorder. Taking them one at a time, you give each a card upon which there is a nursery rhyme or a funny story. They are asked to read these for their recording but to try to disguise their voice.

When the tape is played later in the evening, the guests are given paper and pencil and asked to put the names of the speakers against the numbers provided. Much amusement is caused as the disguised voices are played over the tape, and many will certainly not be recognisable.

The winner is the person who correctly identifies the greatest number of voices.

3

Team Games for Parties

A S these games require a fair amount of energy on the part of your guests it is as well to make this generally known at the outset so that anyone who does not feel up to the exertion may gracefully withdraw and join the spectators.

But for those who are ready to participate, even if only for two or three games, this section offers a number of suggestions for suitable games which are sure to be enjoyed. Some are old, others are quite new, but all have been tried and tested at numerous functions, and voted 'good party games'.

ROMEO AND JULIET

This version of 'Blind Man's Buff' has the great advantage over the original that it is completely safe and there is no risk of your guests tripping over objects in the home and hurting themselves, as can sometimes happen when the players are blindfolded.

Arrange your guests, except for one man and one woman,

in a circle, mixing the ladies among the men as much as possible. The two remaining players then stand back-to-back in the centre of the circle, with the man blindfolded.

When the man calls 'Juliet?', the lady replies 'Here I am, Romeo', whereupon the blindfolded man turns and tries to catch her as she seeks to evade his grasp. If he fails, he again calls 'Juliet' and again the lady must answer, this time saying 'Over here'. All the action takes place within the circle and the man will sometimes think that he has caught Juliet when he touches a member of the outside ring, in which case the person concerned simply answers 'Sorry' and he has to continue the chase.

The aim of the game is for the man to catch Juliet within a time limit set by the host, who should be controlling the game and not participating in it. If the man catches Juliet, he removes his blindfold and hands it over to the lady, who now wears it. Another man is then selected from the group to represent Romeo and stands back-to-back with the lady. A similar procedure is followed, but this time the lady is calling for Romeo and trying to catch him. This can be repeated as many times as desired, and if the blindfolded guest is unable to catch his partner within the time limit, he or she retains the blindfold and another guest is selected to take the place.

Having the group in a circle ensures that the game is confined to a reasonable area, and is also a safeguard against accidents which might otherwise occur. Take care not to let the game go on for too long; leave your guests wanting more, rather than bored or exhausted.

CAT AND MOUSE

An old game, but still a 'must' when planning amusements for large numbers.

Your guests are seated in chairs set against the walls of the room, which has a table, preferably the dining-room table, in the centre.

The host selects two guests, a man and a woman, to start the proceedings. Both are blindfolded and guided towards the table. One represents a cat, the other a mouse, and the object of the game is for the cat to catch the mouse, but under the following conditions. Each player must always have one hand touching the table-top, and when they are guided towards the table neither must know the position of the other. As both cat and mouse have to rely upon their sense of hearing to find or evade one another, it is obviously important that they move as quietly as possible and that the spectators remain silent.

The game commences and both players may move around the table in either direction. They can stop at any time, concentrating for a few seconds to try and hear any movement made by their quarry. If the cat does succeed in catching the mouse within a stated time limit, the partners retire and another two take their places and follow the same procedure.

As explained, the game may sound somewhat 'cold' but, in fact, it provides a lot of fun and excitement for the players, while the other guests find it amusing to watch. Not all your guests need be invited to participate, or the game will go on for too long, but make sure that those left out have the opportunity to participate in other games later on.

FOLLOW THE LEADER

Chairs are arranged in a circle and the guests remain seated. One guest is selected to be the 'guesser' and is requested to leave the room whilst the others decide on a leader amongst the group. When one has been chosen, he starts by slapping his hands on his legs. The other guests follow suit, imitating his actions. The 'guesser' is then asked to come in and stands in the centre of the ring of chairs. His task is to spot the leader, which is obviously difficult at this stage since all the guests are doing exactly the same thing. The leader then changes his actions and begins to clap his hands, and immediately the others follow suit. The 'guesser' must be quick off the mark to see who introduced this change, especially as the leader will try to wait until his back is turned before starting a new action. Each time the leader changes his actions, such as rising from his chair and sitting down again, the others are quick to follow so that once again the entire group are doing the same thing at the same time. If and when the 'guesser' succeeds in identifying the leader, he takes his place within the circle and the leader then becomes the 'guesser'.

IDENTIFYING YOUR PARTNER

Still using chairs in a circle, this next game is a winner at any party, and is also suitable for children.

The guests are divided into two teams. One team leaves the room whilst the others form themselves into a ring, in which there are enough chairs for the total number of both teams. A vacant chair is left beside each member of the 'resident' team, all of whom are blindfolded by their host and left to await the return of the 'visiting' team. When they enter they have a free choice as to where they will sit, and all chairs are finally occupied. At a signal from their host, they all start singing a song, which has been agreed on beforehand. The aim of the game is for the blindfolded guests to identify their neighbours solely by their singing voices. The song over, each blindfolded guest is asked to name his or her partner, and the 'resident' team is awarded one point for each correct identification. They then remove their blindfolds and leave the room, to return later as the 'visiting' team with the chance to score more points than the other team and so win the game.

BALLOON RACE

Based on the popular 'Egg and Spoon' race, this is an excellent team game for children's parties and can be presented either indoors or out.

Two teams of equal numbers are lined up at one end of the room or hall. Two chairs, one for each team, are placed at opposite ends of the lines. The leader starts by placing a balloon on an ordinary tablespoon and, at a given signal, the race begins.

The child must carefully carry the balloon, balanced on the spoon, down to the opposite end of the room, turn around the chair, and return to the next person in line, who then repeats the procedure. This goes on until all the children have participated, and the winning team is the one which first completes the race. If the balloon should fall off the spoon (and indeed it often does) it must be replaced and the player with the spoon returns to his original position and starts again.

PASS THE MATCHBOX

Two teams of even numbers stand in two rows. The leader at the head of each team places the outer cover of the matchbox on his nose and the winning team is the one which, without ever handling the box, successfully passes it along the line to the end of the row, the last player running to the front and holding up his hand. If a box should be allowed to fall during the game, the entire team is disqualified.

MAGIC CIRCLE

A circle of chairs or stools is so formed that a space is left between each. To start with, the players are seated whilst the odd man sits on a separate chair or stool in the centre of the circle. At a signal from the host, the players stand up and move around in a clockwise direction until a whistle is blown, when they must immediately move in the opposite direction.

The object of the game is for the odd man in the centre to obtain one of the vacant chairs as the others are on the move, and quickly sit on it. Players must watch out for this move and quickly retain a chair. The confusing instructions repeatedly given to the guests ensure that the results will be hilarious.

SPOON TROUBLE

A number of spoons, one less than the number of guests playing the game, are arranged in a circle, each a few feet apart. The guests form another circle around the spoons. Music, provided by a tape-recorder or record-player, is played and when this is stopped by the host the guests must quickly stoop to pick up a spoon. One guest must always be the unlucky one and retires from the game; so too, does another spoon. The winner is the last person to remain on the floor with a spoon.

GIFT TROUBLE

This is similar to the game just described, except that

instead of spoons, gifts, wrapped in paper, are stacked in the central position. There should be one gift less than the numbers participating. Each guest rushes forward when the music stops and collects a gift, the unlucky loser retiring from the game. Gifts are replaced, one less each time, and this is repeated until there remains only one guest, who keeps the gift he has collected.

WOOL WINDING

Guests form a circle and remain seated during this game.

Previously, a ball of wool has been wound through and around the legs of each chair, in different directions. Each guest has a separate ball of wool and has to remain seated while he tries to unwind the mass and coil it into a neat round ball. Players are not permitted to stand up or move away from their chairs, and anyone who breaks the wool while unwinding is disqualified. The winner is the one who first succeeds in winding his complete ball of wool.

4

Party Stunts

THE following stunts collected by the author will be found useful 'fillers' for the occasional dull moment in a party when conversation tends to flag and something is needed to liven things up. They are not conjuring tricks, since they have no real secrets, and no skill or prior preparations are required for their presentation.

As well as being suitable for parties in the home, they can also be effectively introduced on other social occasions, such as in a hotel or at a bar, and they are the more baffling in that most involve only common articles in everyday use.

TWO INTO ONE WILL GO

This party stunt seems impossible and when your guests try it for themselves few will be successful.

The aim of the experiment is for the guest to remove two coins balancing on the edge of a tumbler, using only two fingers. It can be done, and the illustrations on page 17 show just how. The coins are balanced on the edge opposite to each other. The index finger and thumb of the right hand comes over towards the coins and press firmly down. The coins 'snap' against the side of the tumbler and so can be taken away towards the central position. The fingers then quickly draw the coins towards the body, where they are firmly held together with the two fingers.

STRONG NOTE

Can one really break a pencil with a borrowed £1 note or a dollar bill? Certainly it appears to be possible and the only apparatus needed is a pencil and a note.

The note is folded lengthwise in half as shown in Figure 1 and you ask someone to hold the pencil firmly between his hands. Then, as you bring the folded note down to strike the pencil, you extend your index finger and with one sharp blow the pencil is broken in half. Of course, the finger is actually doing the work, but it looks exactly as if the note were responsible for the 'break'.

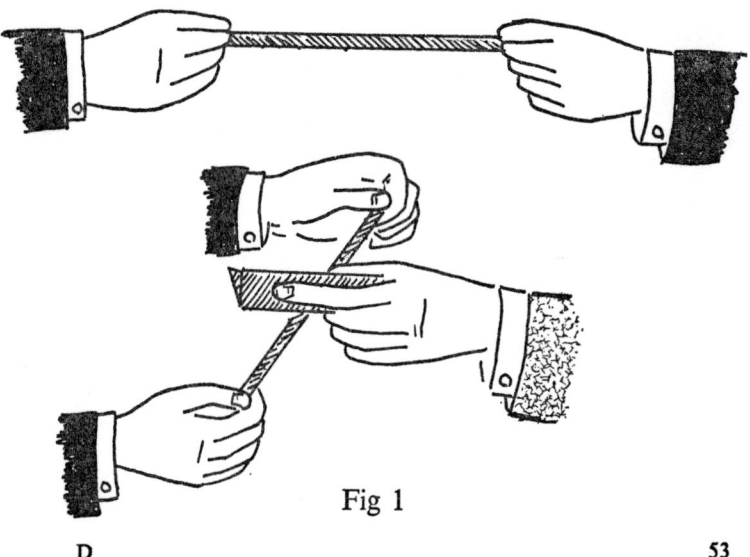

Fig 1

SNAP A MATCH

Few of your guests will believe they are not strong enough to snap a common match between their fingers but if you ask them to hold it as shown in the illustration on page 18 no matter how hard they try, they will not succeed in breaking it. A great deal of fun, and considerable surprise, will be caused by this simple experiment and all your other guests will want to try it.

CIGARETTE CIRCLE

This is an appropriate stunt to introduce when offering cigarettes to your guests. Ask if anyone can bend a cigarette round in a circle without breaking it? It can be done but, unless the guest knows the trick, it will be advisable to let him experiment with his own cigarettes! The answer is as simple as it is effective. Wrap the cigarette in a piece of

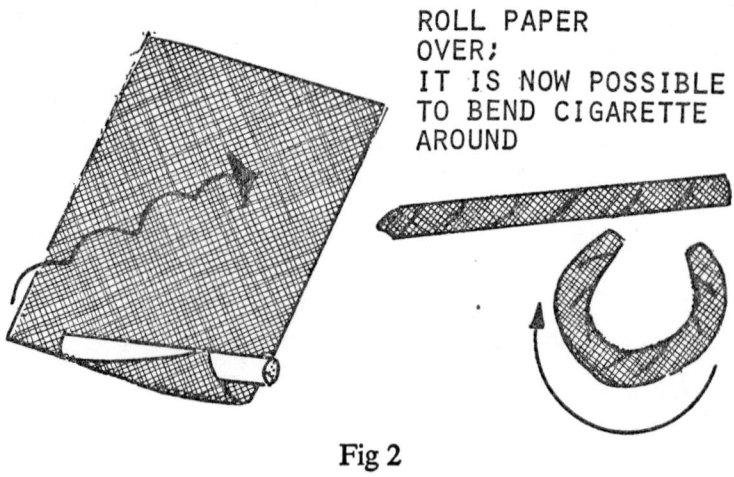

ROLL PAPER OVER;
IT IS NOW POSSIBLE TO BEND CIGARETTE AROUND

Fig 2

clear cellophane, rolling it inside. When completely covered, the cigarette can be bent round to form a circle, without damaging it in any way.

CRAZY PEG

A small metal or wooden peg is produced and is shown to be impossible to balance on the tip of the finger. Guests may try, but will not succeed. You then offer to show how it can be done and say that to make the feat even more difficult, you will use a heavy strap as well. This is wedged into the central position where it hangs at an angle. Because of the way in which the peg has been cut, you will find it possible to balance it, plus the strap, on the very edge of your finger—an apparently remarkable achievement as the illustration on page 18 shows.

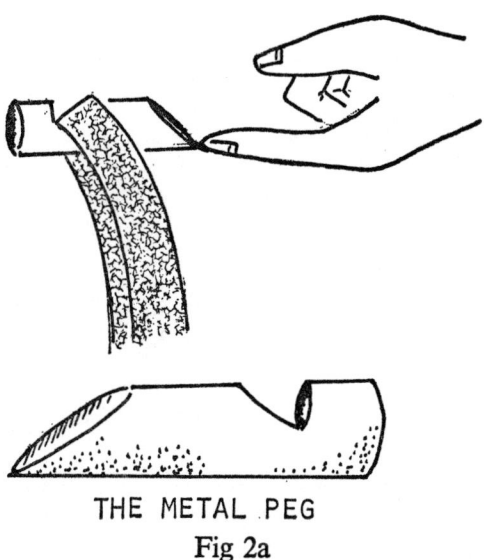

THE METAL PEG
Fig 2a

LARGE THROUGH SMALL

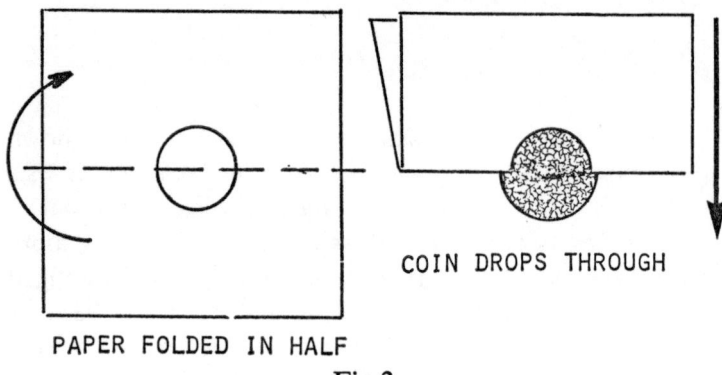

COIN DROPS THROUGH

PAPER FOLDED IN HALF

Fig 3

Take a square of paper with a hole in its centre which is obviously smaller than the diameter of the 10p piece or similar large coin you propose to use. Ask your guests if they think it possible to push the coin through the hole, and when they assure you that it is not, fold the paper in half and drop the coin into the hole. Then, holding both sides of the paper, bend these up and the coin will fall through.

TURN-ABOUT ARROW

This is a stunt which I recently presented on television for a party programme, when it aroused much interest.

Given a square piece of cardboard on which a bold arrow has been drawn, the object of the experiment is to make the arrow turn in the opposite direction without reversing the card.

Pick up a glass of water and if you place this in front of the card, the arrow automatically reverses itself—a simple optical illusion. The second part of the experiment,

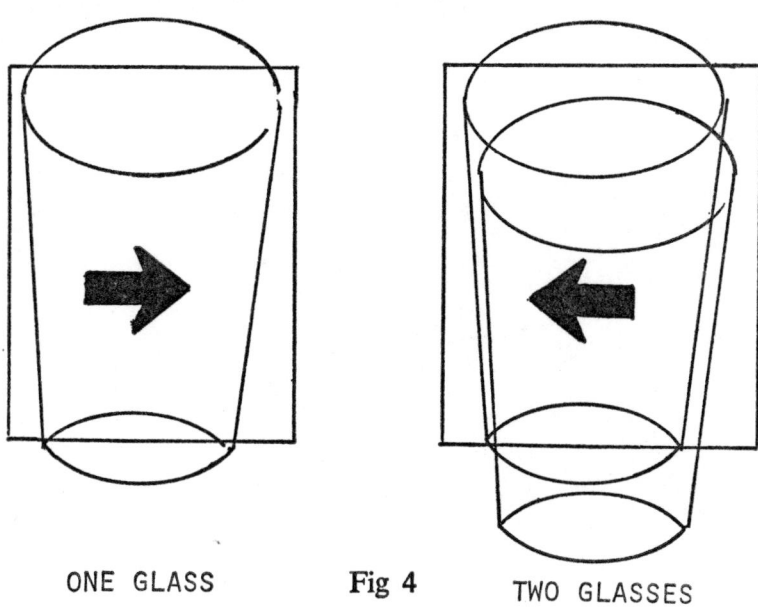

ONE GLASS   **Fig 4**   TWO GLASSES

you then say, is more difficult, the object being to reverse
the position of the arrow again without removing the glass
or touching the card. When your audience admits that they
have no idea how this can be achieved, place another tumbler of water in front of the first and the arrow will immediately appear to have returned to its original position.

BALANCING MATCH

Ask someone to try and balance a match upright, head
down, on a piece of paper, and he will surely fail unless,
like you, he knows the secret of the trick. This is secretly
to place a little saliva on the head of the match so that
when the head is pushed firmly down onto the paper the
match stays upright for some time. It looks incredible and
the 'steadiness' of your hand will be much admired.

Fig 5

A HOLE IN THE HAND

Fig 6

That's exactly what it looks like when you present this piece of party entertainment. A length of cartridge paper is used and formed in to a roll. The right hand is held upright, palm towards your face as shown in the diagram opposite. The tube is placed against this and when the spectator looks through it, there will indeed appear to be a hole running right through your hand.

CLIP-LINK

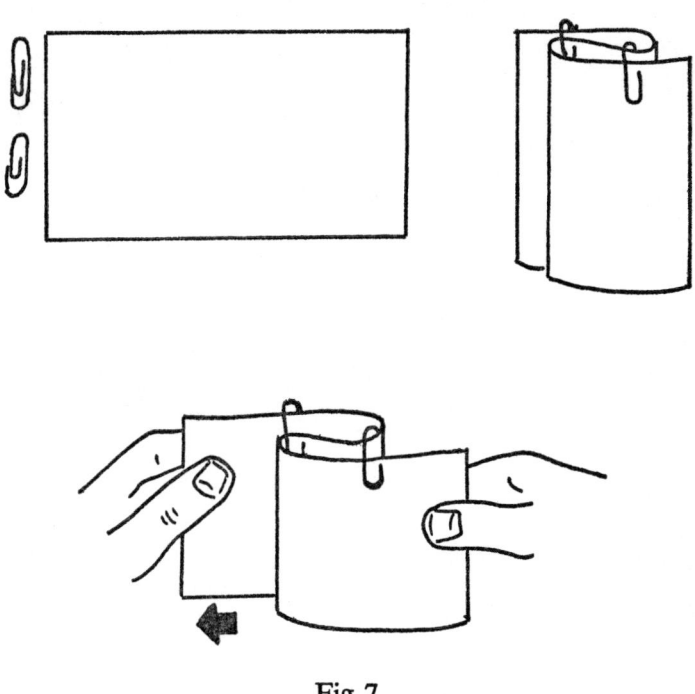

Fig 7

This is an effective and amusing stunt which your guests will surely want to adopt for their own parties. All that is required is a £1 note or dollar bill, or any piece of paper money, plus two ordinary paper clips. The clips are placed at the positions shown in the diagram (Fig 7). When the note is pulled from each side, the clips spookily run along to join each other in the centre and become linked—and genuinely linked, too.

COIN BRIDGE

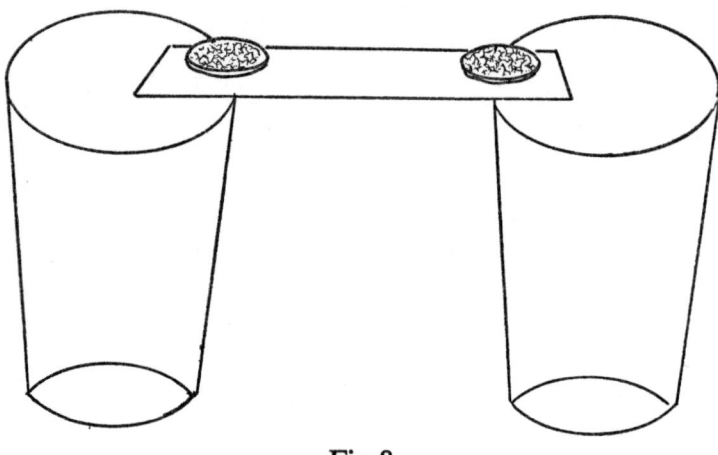

Fig 8

With a strip of paper placed between two tumblers and two coins balanced on the edge of each glass, on top of the paper, you are all set to offer another problem to your guests. The objective is to remove the strip of paper without dislodging the coins. It sounds impossible but, again, is quite simple—when you know the secret.

Slightly moisten your finger and, with one downward move, strike the paper from the top position in the centre. You will then find that the paper *can* be removed, leaving the coins in their original positions.

MATCH WALK

A dinner-table stunt, this, in which you can show how two matches can be made to walk along a table-knife without visible help.

First cut a cleft in the end of one match and sharpen the

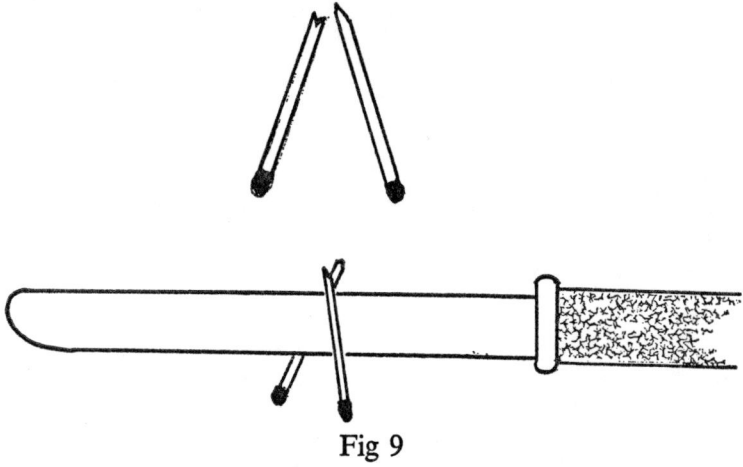

Fig 9

other end of the second. Fit the matches together to form a V shape and slide them on to the end of the knife as shown in the diagram. Hold the knife parallel to the table-top with one end slightly up, and by constantly shaking the knife a little, both matches will be made to walk smartly from one end of the blade to the other.

MAGNETIC MATCH

In this old but always effective stunt a match is placed head uppermost onto the arm, from which it jumps up into the air. The trick can be successfully repeated as many times

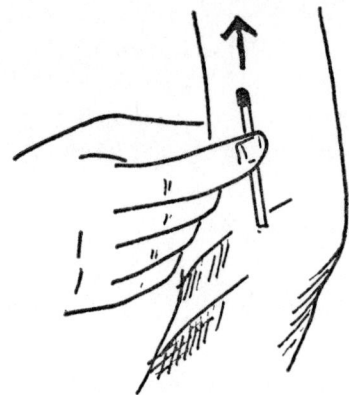

Fig 10

as you wish and though all your guests will want to have a try, few will succeed in bringing it off.

The secret is to hold your arm right in front of you and to place the match on a tight fold of cloth on your jacket or garment. You then merely press down on the match and up it will jump. The most effective method of presentation is to make several purposely unsuccessful attempts as a build-up to the successful climax.

THREE AT A TIME

Fig 11

Ask if anyone can pick up three matches with one match? It can be done, and here is the secret. Arrange three matches to form a tripod as shown in the diagram. If you then light the heads of all three matches, they will become bonded together and can be lifted off the table by another match.

PENNY AND POUND

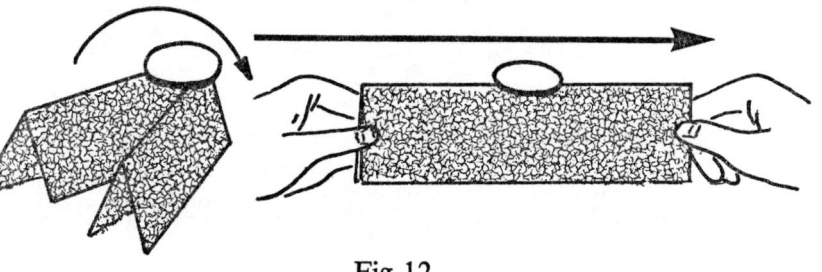

Fig 12

To balance a penny on the edge of a pound note, first fold the note in half lengthwise, and then fold the folded note in half, as shown in the diagram. Now place the coin in the centre of 'V shape' of the note and with both hands, one on each side, draw it apart and you will find that the coin will remain on the edge of the note.

A LONG FINGER

In this stunt you can make it appear to anyone that one of your fingers is at least an inch longer than the others.

To accomplish this, use your left-hand index finger. The right-hand index finger is allowed to pull in so that the next finger is pushed up to it. The nail being covered underneath the curled finger, what looks like one longer finger is seen. The illustration on page 18 shows how realistic this can appear and the hand movements are shown in Fig 12a overleaf.

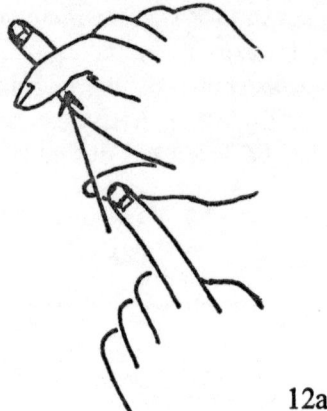

12a

LIFTING A BOTTLE WITH A STRAW

SHOWING STRAW
WEDGED INSIDE
BOTTLE

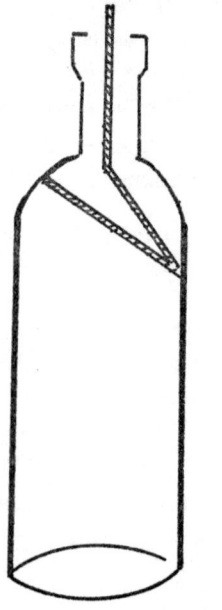

Fig 13

The problem here is for your guests to lift a bottle off the table with an ordinary straw, without tying it around the neck or putting it under the bottle.

After they have been given time to try and solve the problem, you sharply bend the straw about one-third up from the bottom and lower it into the bottle. When pulled upright, the straw will engage against the shoulder of the bottle and so enable the bottle to be lifted clear of the table.

MAGIC PAPER

This is a party stunt in which all can participate. Give everyone a piece of paper and tell them to write in capital

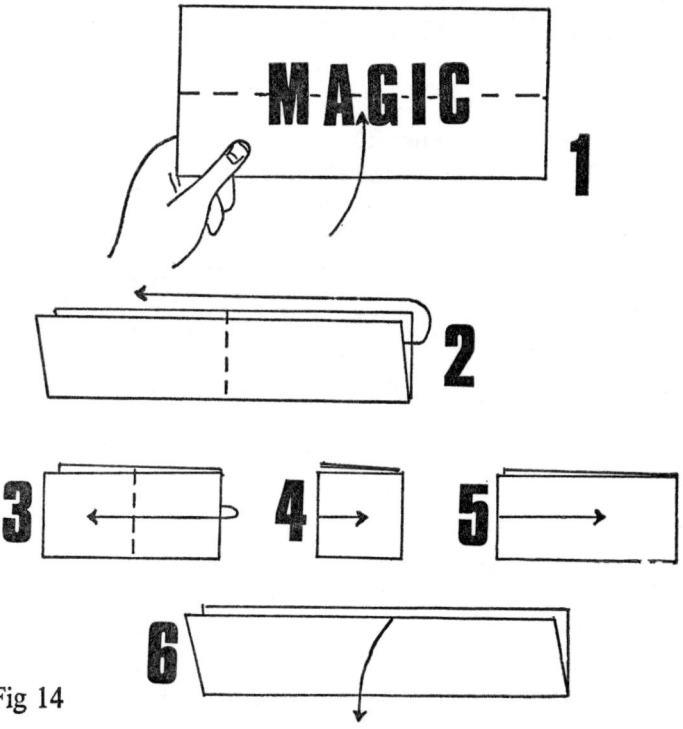

Fig 14

letters the word 'MAGIC' right in the centre. Or you may prefer to have the papers already prepared, with the word neatly stencilled on.

The piece of paper is folded several times and, when re-opened, the word 'MAGIC' appears upside down. At no time during the foldings does the paper appear to get reversed yet the word always comes out the wrong way up.

The secret, of course, is in the method of folding, illustrated in Fig 14.

First hold the paper as shown in '1' and fold in half as indicated by dashes and arrow.

2 When folded, fold again from right to left as shown.
3 The result. Fold from right to left again but in front position.
4 The result. Commence to reopen the paper. Open right side out.
5 The result. Now follow the arrow again, opening to the right once more. The paper appears to be similar to '2', but when opened downwards as at '6' the word 'MAGIC' is now reversed. Truly a word of mystery.

PAPER LADDERS AND TREES

Making ladders and trees from rolls of coloured paper is one of the most popular of all paper-tearing stunts, and can produce some fine examples well suited for use as Christmas decorations. It can also be used to good effect as a competition for a children's party, the child making the tallest tree or ladder being the winner.

Both trees and ladders are easy to make and the procedure will speedily be grasped after a study of the accompanying diagrams.

Begin by arranging the various sheets of coloured wrappings or poster paper. To the edge of one piece paste another, preferably of a different colour to make things more interesting. Continue doing this until you have one large roll and then paste the edge of the outside sheet to form a self-contained cylinder.

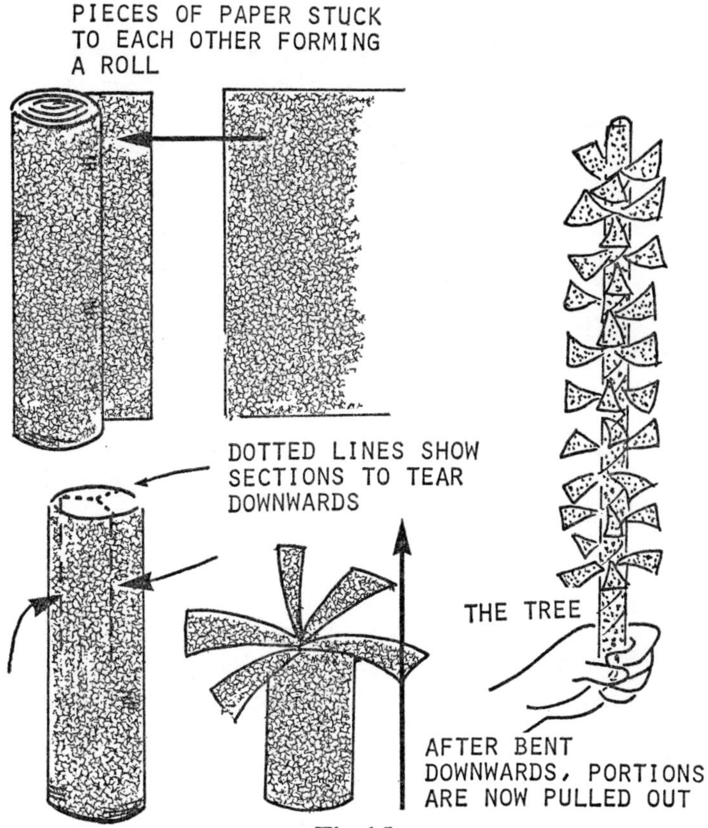

PIECES OF PAPER STUCK
TO EACH OTHER FORMING
A ROLL

DOTTED LINES SHOW
SECTIONS TO TEAR
DOWNWARDS

THE TREE

AFTER BENT
DOWNWARDS, PORTIONS
ARE NOW PULLED OUT

Fig 15

The Tree: With a pair of sharp scissors, cut through the layers as illustrated, so there will be quite a number of loose strips towards the top. By pulling the inside upwards, the tree is formed and the hanging strips blossom forth as branches.

The Ladder: The same basic procedure is followed and the dotted lines shown in the diagram indicate the portion which has to be cut out. When this has been removed, the

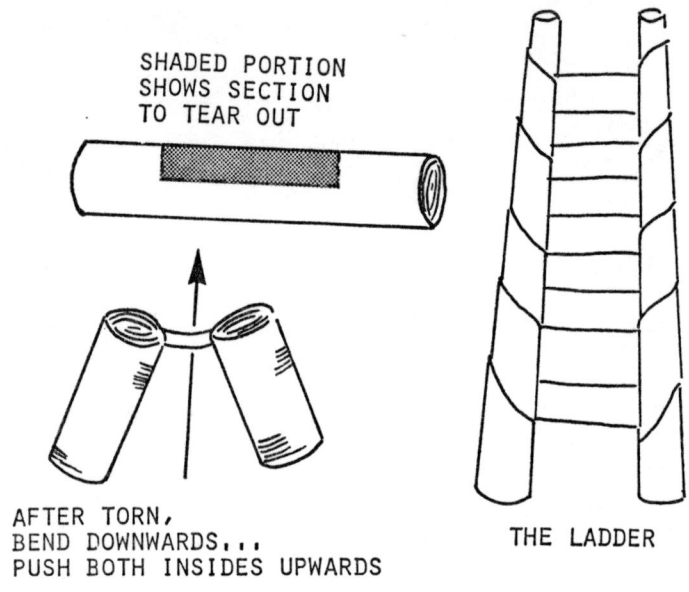

SHADED PORTION
SHOWS SECTION
TO TEAR OUT

AFTER TORN,
BEND DOWNWARDS...
PUSH BOTH INSIDES UPWARDS

THE LADDER

Fig 16

roll is bent over so that two stalks take shape and the centre portion is forced upwards. These strips form the rungs of the ladder. The picture on page 35 shows a completed ladder and tree.

5

Origami for your Guests

ORIGAMI is the Japanese word for paper folding. The Japanese are famous for their intricate folds resulting in charming paper dolls and tokens and most attractive wrappings. Origami is an art, and many 'folders' in all parts of the world take it very seriously. In Britain, Robert Harbin, an expert and author of many fine works on the subject, leads the field and his creations, beautifully illustrated and detailed, are true examples of perfect Origami.

The following examples can be made by anyone, and although at first some may seem complicated, they are, in fact, all easy to master. With some guidance from their host or hostess, party guests should have no difficulty in producing smart table decorations, party hats, designs and competition models, and all will find the pastime both fascinating and relaxing.

The paper used should be of good quality, thin but strong. Origami paper is obtainable from handicraft shops, and can be purchased in packets already cut to the correct size. It is normally coloured on one side only. If you cannot

E

obtain this paper, various kinds of wrapping papers, or even brown paper may be used. The papers must, however, be cut accurately, just as the folds must be perfect if your final models are to reach an acceptable standard. Robert Harbin prefers his papers to be 17.5cm square, 14.5cm square, and 12cm square.

The first requirement is to get to know the various standard symbols used in Origami folding. These are based on Akira Yoshizawa's and Robert Harbin's codes of lines and arrows, and I am most grateful to Robert Harbin for his permission to describe here his own methods and creations.

Origami has to be explained by illustrations and the separate drawings, each one blending into the next phase, show the reader step by step how a model is formed.

Let us now study the symbols used by Origami folders. Your party guests will find the instructions easy to follow if you first explain and demonstrate the various folds in front of them.

ORIGAMI SYMBOLS

Valley Fold
This is indicated by a line of dashes. As shown on the accompanying diagram, the paper is folded downwards.
Mountain Fold
This is indicated by a series of dots and dashes. In this case, the paper is folded backwards (see diagram).
To Crease
A thin line is drawn to show a crease.
Turn Over
A specially designed arrow shows how the model should be turned over.
Fold Over and Over
Indicated by a caterpillar arrow.

ORIGAMI SYMBOLS

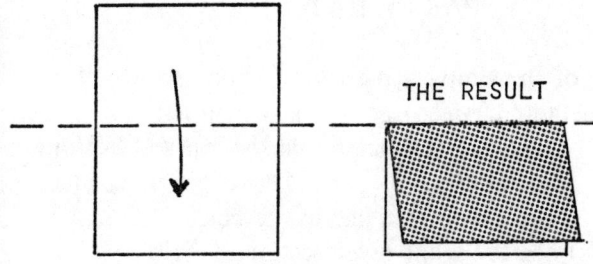

VALLEY FOLD DOTS AND DASHES

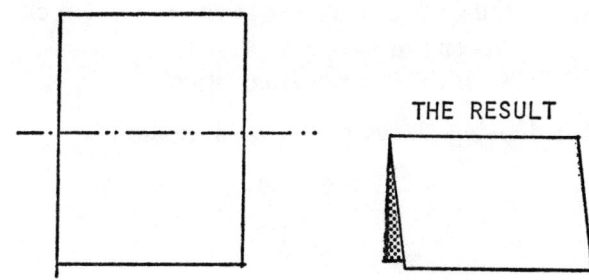

MOUNTAIN FOLD DOTS AND DASHES

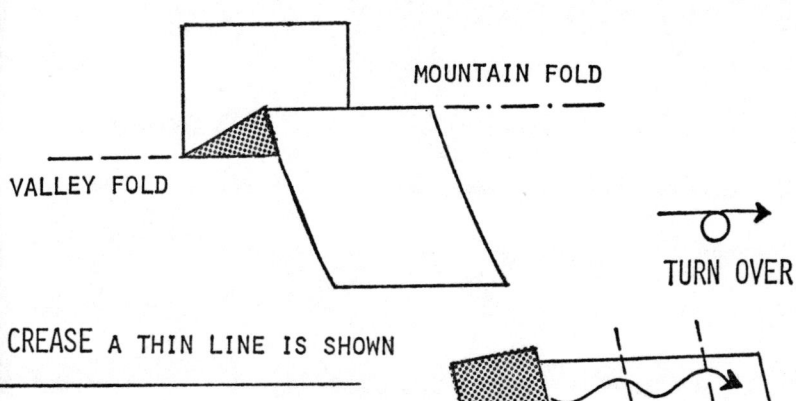

CREASE A THIN LINE IS SHOWN

Fig 17

FOLD OVER AND OVER A CATERPILLAR ARROW

PARTY HAT

This is one of the simplest models to make, so it will be our first. A rectangular piece of paper is required.

Diagram 1 As shown, mountain-fold the top and bottom corners of the paper. Their edges must meet along the centre line in the back.

Diagram 2 Fold the front layer section in half.

Diagram 3 Arrow shows how to fold in half, and when the triangular shape is formed make sure its end is tucked into the centre portion. Now mountain-fold the remaining triangle, tucking its end in similarly.

Diagram 4 Open out the crown from below.

The shaded drawing shows the finished model.

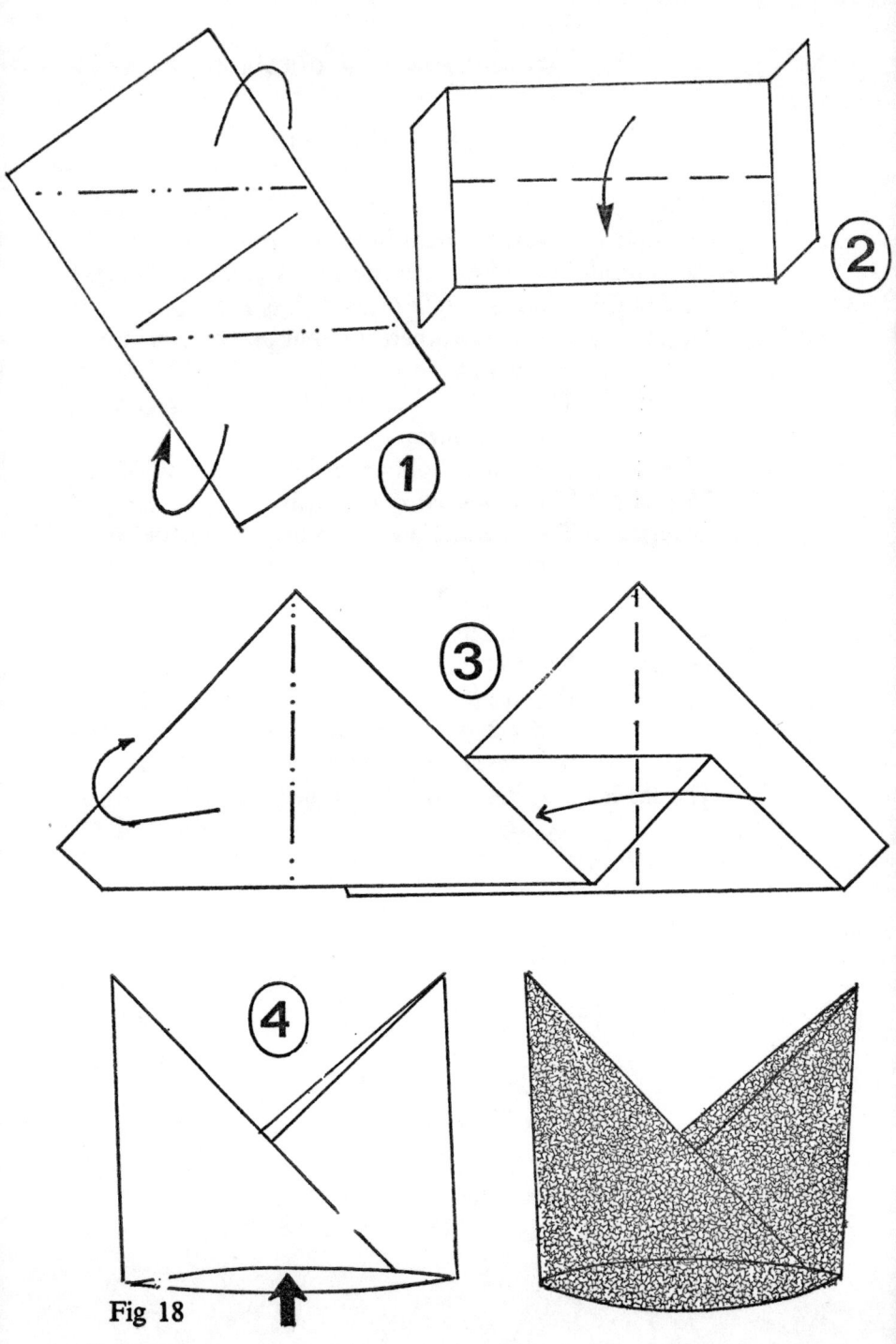

Fig 18

A SMART BOW TIE

Take a piece of paper, and with a few slick folds, surprise your guests by transforming it into a beautiful bow tie. The finished result looks most realistic and is produced entirely from a single square of paper measuring 6in by $2\frac{3}{4}$in.

Diagram 1 Fold the corners to central position, using valley-folds as shown.

Diagram 2 The result. Once again fold along the dotted lines as shown.

Diagram 3 The result. Fold paper in half as indicated.

Diagram 4 Mountain-fold downwards.

Diagram 5 The result. Follow the arrow and fold both flaps upwards.

Diagram 6 The result. Fold the two bottom corners following arrows.

Diagram 7 Place both forefingers (one on each side) at the position marked 'X', and with the thumbs under flaps 'A' and 'B' open these up, exerting pressure between thumbs and forefingers.

The shaded drawing shows the finished model.

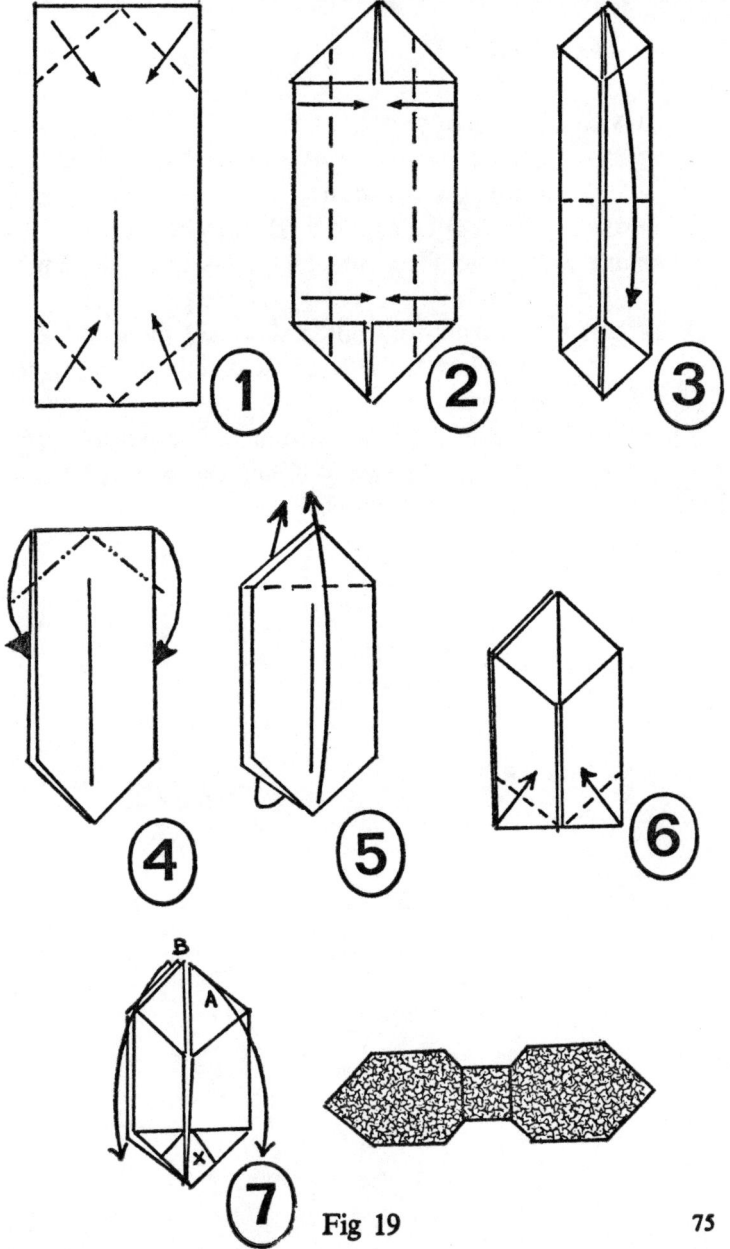

Fig 19

LIGIA MONTOYA'S FISH

Start with a square of paper.

Diagram 1 Crease the paper as shown. Valley-fold the top flap downwards.

Diagram 2 The result. Now turn the model over.

Diagram 3 Mountain-fold the two sides into the centre crease.

Diagram 4 Mountain-fold and valley-fold flaps 'A' and 'B'. The points shown will sink and move to the centre.

Diagram 5 Here is the new position. Now cut a slit in the tail. Reverse-fold tail pieces twice each.

Diagram 6 The result. Now turn the model over.

Diagram 7 The completed model.

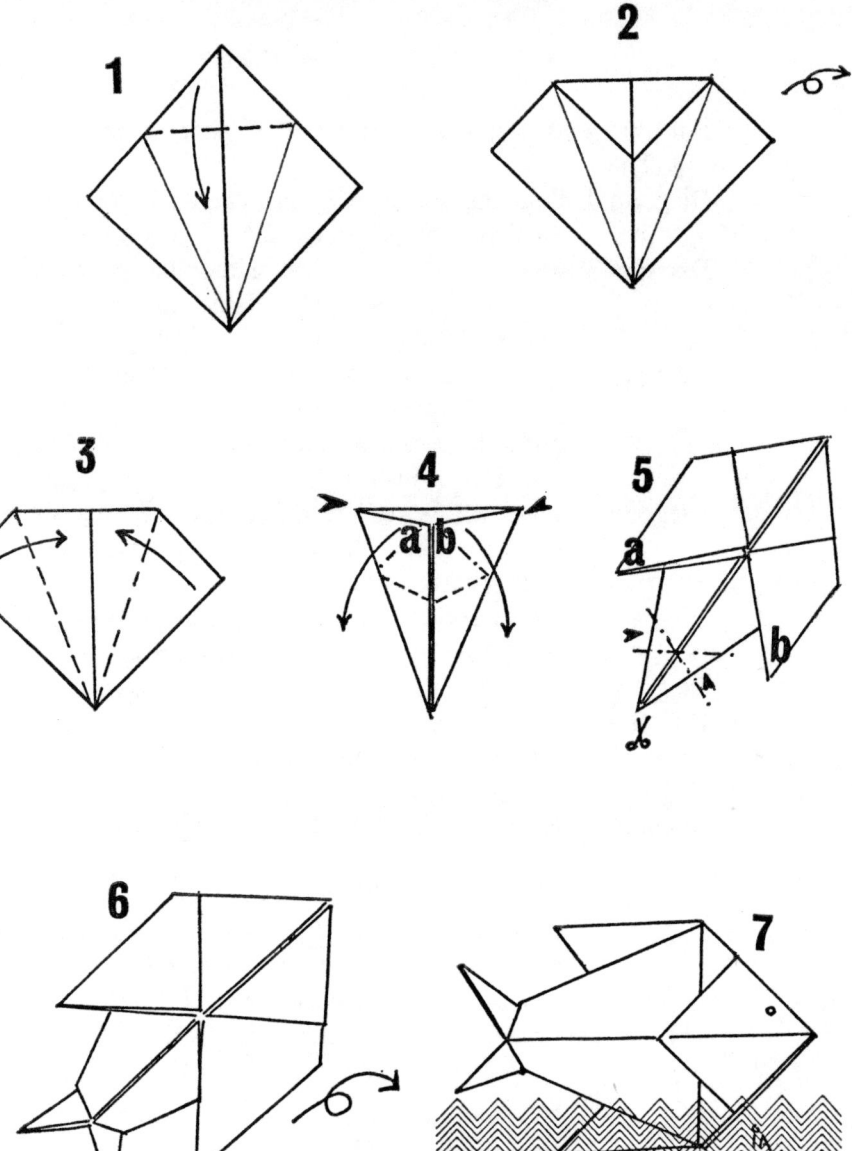

Fig 20

SIGNET RING (Neal Elias)

For this fold you require a piece of paper measuring 6in by 2¾in.

Diagram 1 Fold the top corners downwards as one and then fold the model in half.

Diagram 2 First valley-fold the left side of the paper at an angle as shown. Mountain-fold the opposite as shown.

Diagram 3 The result. Valley-fold the left side of the paper, bringing it back to the horizontal position. Next mountain-fold the complete centre strip in half.

Diagram 4 This will be the result. Form the ring by bending round the right side of the band, ending with a semicircle.

Diagram 5 Arrow shows how to bend the left side of the band over to the right, making a circle.

Diagram 6 The result. Fold the top part downwards.

Diagram 7 Your paper should look like this. Now mountain-fold the lower part through the actual ring.

Diagram 8 At this position, fold in both tips as illustrated.

Diagram 9 Finally the right protruding end is folded right over, first folding in the tip so that it will engage into the ring, very much like a standard flap of an envelope.

The shaded drawing displays the finished ring.

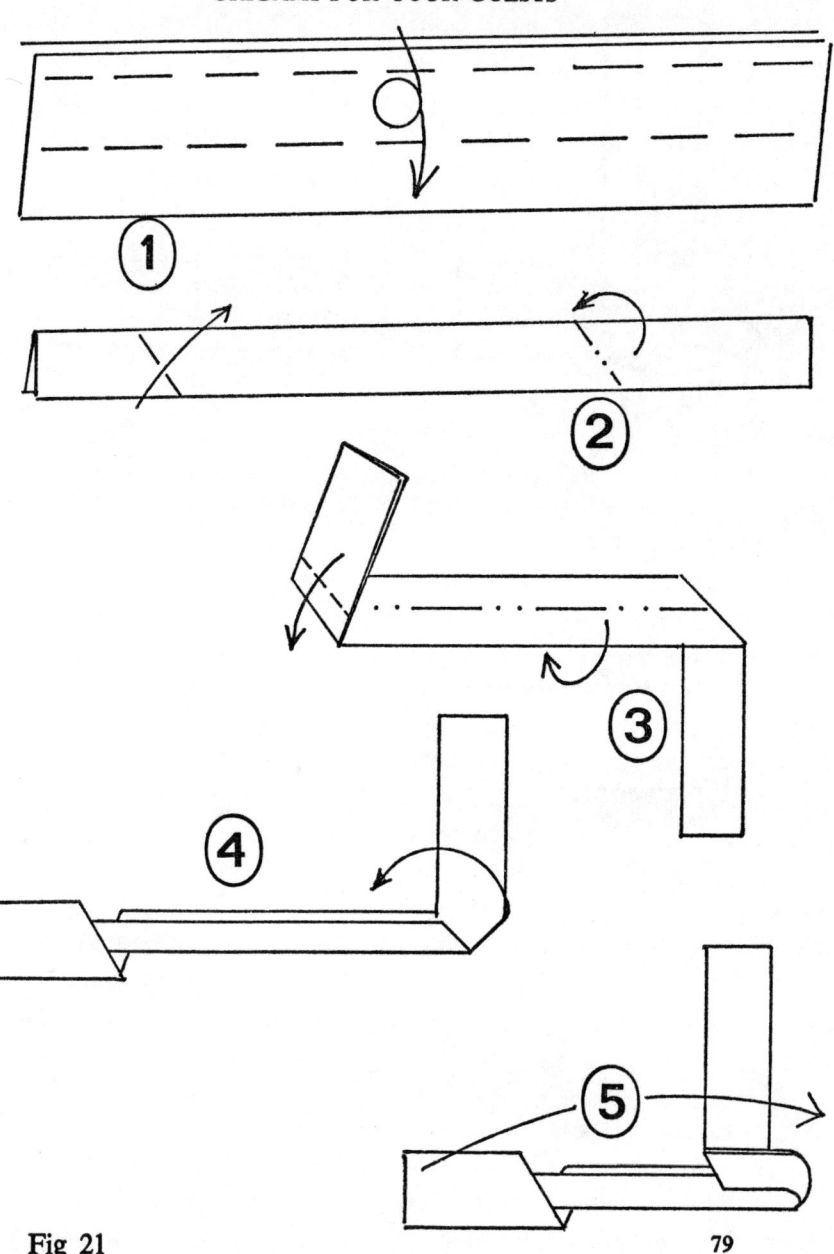

Fig 21

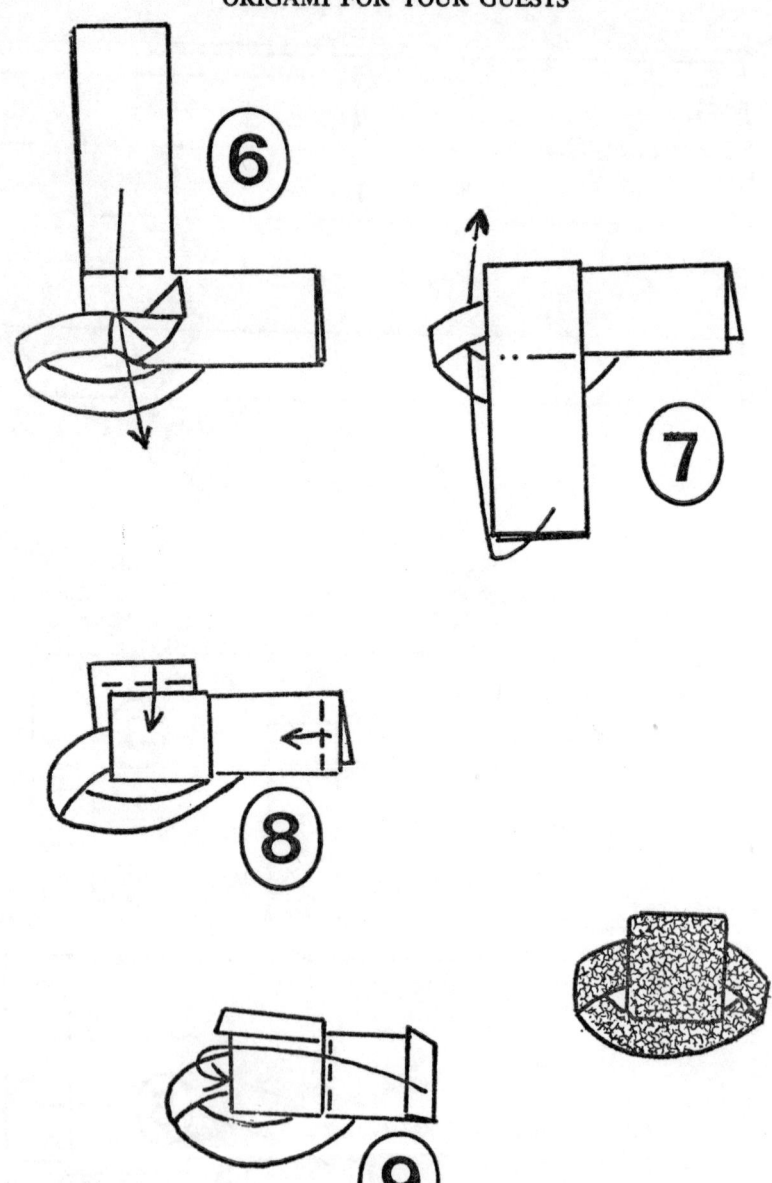

Fig 21a

THE FLAPPING BIRD

An old Japanese model this, but one which is extremely popular. When completed, as shown overleaf, the bird almost comes to life and when its tail is pulled, the wings flap as though it were about to take flight.

Diagram 1 Start with a piece of square paper. Crease as shown in the illustration.

Diagram 2 Mountain-fold corners 'A' and 'B'.

Diagram 3 The result. Valley-fold to form illustration.

Diagram 4 Valley-fold as shown, crease, then unfold back to illustration 3 again.

Diagram 5 Mountain-fold (dots and dashes). Lift flap 'C' in the direction of the arrow. Illustration 6 shows how the model is taking shape. Do this on both sides.

Diagram 6 The result.

Diagram 7 Upper flap is folded from left to right, as shown by the arrow. Repeat this on the other side.

Diagram 8 The result so far. The flap is folded upwards and indicated by the arrow, both sides.

Diagram 9 The result. Hold gently at position 'O' with thumb and forefinger. Pull corner 'A' down in the direction of the arrow until it is positioned as in diagram 10.

Diagram 10 One side has been brought down. The opposite side is also brought down. Mountain-fold the position 'A' to form head as illustrated.

Hold the model between finger and thumb at breast position, and if the tail is pulled, the bird's wings will flap. (See illustration on page 35.)

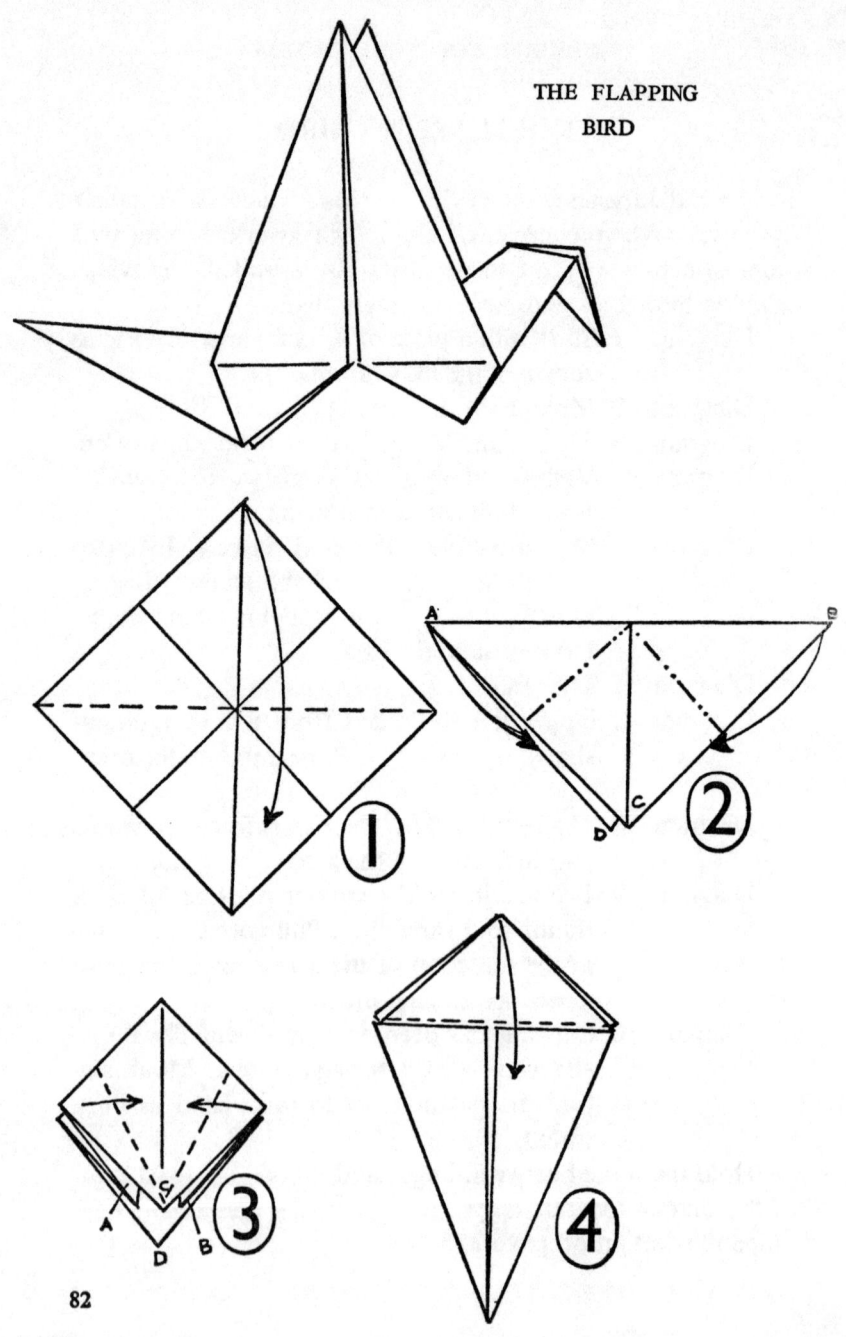

THE FLAPPING
BIRD

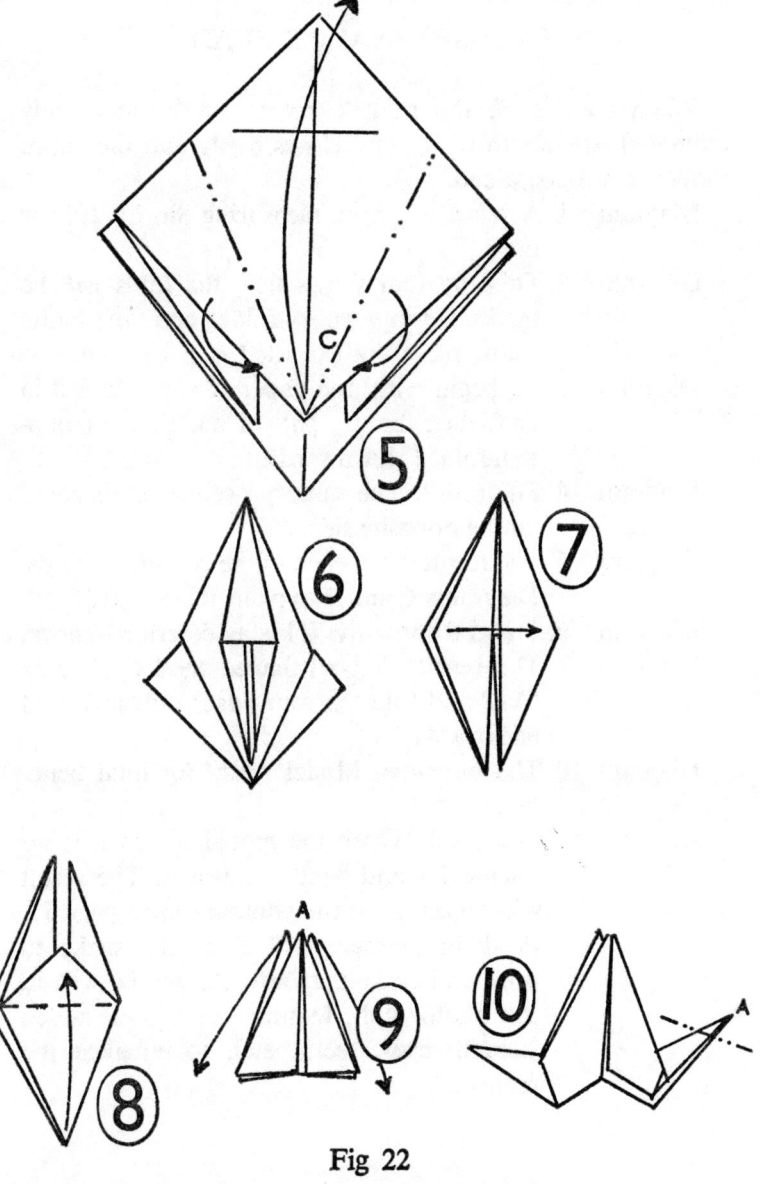

Fig 22

Fig 23

TALKING SNAKE'S HEAD

When completed, the snake's head, can be amusingly animated. Its mouth opens and closes easily and the entire model is self-contained.

Diagram 1 A piece of paper measuring 8in by 10in is used.

Diagram 2 This diagram shows how the folds *will* be made. Using valley-folds and mountain folds, these are executed step by step.

Diagram 3 To begin with, the paper is valley-folded in half, then the top part of one side is mountain-folded downwards.

Diagram 4 The result. The same procedure is repeated on the opposite side.

Diagram 5 The result. Fold each of the corners inwards. Diagrams 6 and 7 explain these folds.

Diagram 6, 7 and 8 show the folds as described above.

Diagram 9 The result. A boat-shaped model. Tear at 'AA' and fold the four edges outwards and backwards.

Diagram 10 The outcome. Model ready for final bending.

Diagram 11 The result. Open the model out so it is no longer flat and bend it inwards. The result will appear as in the photograph on page 35. A slight pressure will allow the snake to open and close its mouth. As will be seen in the photograph, features have been added (mouth, eyes, teeth, etc), to enhance the realism.

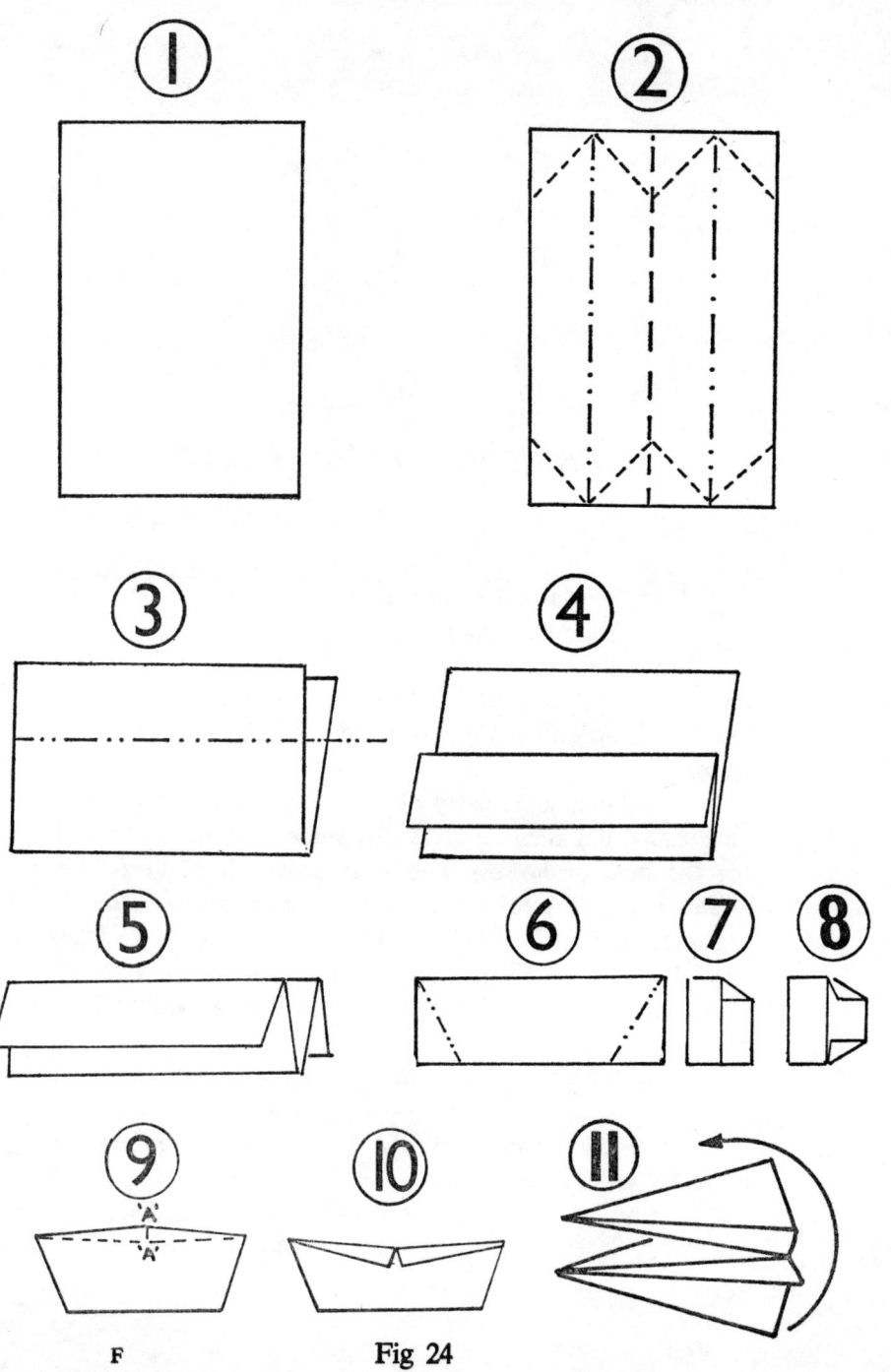

F

Fig 24

6

Conjuring for the Party

A T any social event, and especially at a private party or children's function, conjuring can help to provide excellent entertainment for the guests. And if you, the host, are presenting the 'magic', this will make it even more exciting and the entertainment much more of a surprise.

It is true that some party planners do engage professional 'magicians' but their services can sometimes be costly and for the host or hostess who does not wish to incur this extra expense the following conjuring effects can easily be mastered and will be enjoyed by everyone. All have been specially designed for this book, and as none has previously appeared in print, in this manner, they will be new to most people.

First, a few hints on presenting tricks at a party or social event.

Practise the effect until you know you can present it correctly without fumbling.

Never repeat a trick unless it has been designed for this purpose.

Never reveal the secret of a trick after its performance. An audience is often disappointed when it knows the secret of an illusion and the entertainment value is thereby diminished.

Party tricks are best performed using common objects such as anyone might find around the home. That is why this selection contains tricks with household articles.

It is advisable, and much more entertaining, if your tricks are accompanied by 'patter', or a running commentary. This helps to make a 'trick' and enables the performer to put over his personality.

Your audience should always ask for more, so the wise host takes care not to bore his guests with too long a succession of tricks.

MARKED CARD

Our first conjuring effect requires a pack of genuine playing cards, which may be borrowed from a spectator if necessary. Thus the trick can be presented at any time, and at any party, without prior preparation.

THE TRICK

A pack of cards is displayed and a spectator is given a free choice of selecting any card.

The remainder of the pack is then gathered together and given to yet another spectator who is asked to place the chosen card on top of the pack. Further, he is requested to cut the pack as many times as he wishes until this card is lost amongst the others. It is now obviously impossible for anyone to know its position in the pack.

The performer now collects the pack and fans out the cards. A postage stamp, or an adhesive spot, is produced and the performer sticks this onto the back of one card. The cards are then shuffled so that this card cannot be found and the entire pack is spread, face uppermost, on top of a table.

The spectator is asked to look for *his* selected card and to stick a duplicate stamp, or spot, onto its face. However, when he reverses his card, he finds that there is already a stamp on the opposite side, and on this card alone. 'Great minds think alike, Ladies and Gentlemen' says the performer, as he hands out the pack of cards for examination.

THE WORKING AND PRESENTATION

A subtle twist to an old method here achieves a novel effect, and because the working is simple the performer has time to concentrate on the 'presentation' of the trick.

Start by displaying the cards in a fan. Keep the faces hidden whilst a spectator selects a card. When the card has been chosen and removed, square up the cards into a pack.

The secret is to note and remember the top card of the pack. This can be done while the cards are being displayed after they have been shuffled by a spectator at the start of the trick.

Knowing this card, when the chosen one is placed on top of the pack by the spectator, you can immediately locate it, even after the cards have been cut over and over again. This cutting of the cards does not affect the working of the trick and greatly enhances its presentation, for the audience is convinced that the chosen card must surely have been lost among the others. When the pack is finally returned to you, fan the cards out, watching for the position of the card which once was your top one. The chosen card will always be to the right of this 'locator' card. As soon as you spot it, stick the postage stamp on the back of the card, shuffle the cards thoroughly, pass the pack to the spectator and ask him to spread the cards face up on the table and stick his stamp on the face of his chosen card. When he has done this ask him to turn the card over. Show the audience that it is the card you have already 'marked' on the back and invite the spectator to examine the rest of the pack to satisfy himself that no others have been similarly marked.

LIGHTED CANDLE PENETRATION

This item, like the others in this section, has been specially designed for readers of this book, so that the host who presents it will have something just that little bit different from any other tricks his guests may have seen.

The performer displays a box of matches and removes the tray, emptying out the contents. The box is an ordinary one, except for the hole which has been cut, and runs directly through the outside drawer. The inside tray is quite solid and complete. The matchbox is handed out for examination, after which the matches are replaced and the drawer is pushed into its correct position.

A candle is lit and then suddenly pushed through the bottom of the box. It 'magically' penetrates the solid tray and the matches and comes out at the top, still alight. While the bewildered audience is trying to puzzle out how the candle managed to penetrate the box they had all examined, the candle is removed, The flame blown out, and the box of matches again offered for thorough examination.

THE SECRET

Although a simple method is employed—and many such secrets are simple ones—the working and presentation are unique.

The drawings show you how to prepare the matchbox so that it will be ready for you to use, anytime and anywhere.

Take the outside cover and with a sharp knife, cut a hole through both top and bottom layers. Make sure the cut-outs are slightly larger than the candle used in the effect. The inside drawer is left unfaked. Have a supply of matches already inside.

One final and most important item which I have called 'the gimmick' (magicians' term for an unseen accessory) is a piece of wood which fits into the end of the outside cover.

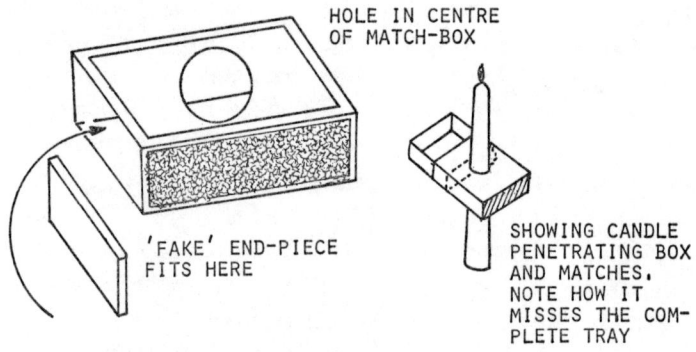

HOLE IN CENTRE OF MATCH-BOX

'FAKE' END-PIECE FITS HERE

SHOWING CANDLE PENETRATING BOX AND MATCHES, NOTE HOW IT MISSES THE COMPLETE TRAY

Fig 25

When this has been painted grey to match the colour of the side of a genuine matchbox tray, the box appears to be closed whereas, in fact, when this piece is flush with the edge of the outside drawer, the opposite end is protruding. (See sketch above.)

This means that when the genuine protruding section is secretly pulled back, the faked end will stay in the same position and the matchbox will appear to be closed. The working of the effect may now become rather obvious but let me explain the correct method of handling the items.

At the commencement, the 'gimmick' is secretly retained

in the hand. No one will know it is there and you must not appear to be conscious of it.

The matchbox is handed out to a spectator for examination and he is requested to open the inside tray and empty the matches. The performer emphasises that the base of the tray is solid whilst the outside cover has a hole in both parts, running right through. The reason for this, you will explain later.

The matches are replaced and the inside tray slid into the outside case, the 'gimmick', meanwhile, being retained unnoticed in your right hand. The fact that you are using this hand during the displaying of the items used, makes it easier for you to 'palm' it. Whilst the inside tray is being secured in position, the 'gimmick' is introduced into one end. The left hand holding the match-box covers the fact that part of the box protrudes. The 'gimmick', when in position, should be flush with the end of the matchbox cover. The left hand should retain a firm grip of this protruding portion whilst the right pulls the tray still further out, leaving the centre holes clear. This is shown clearly in the drawing. The candle standing in its holder on your table is now lit and is removed and then slowly pushed through the hole at the bottom of the box until it passes completely through, making its appearance at the top. The performer explains that the candle is obviously penetrating the inside tray as well as the live matches.

The candle may be removed from the top or if wished, drawn back through the box once more, ending in its original position, underneath the box.

During this procedure, the end of the box has been in view at all times, and the audience imagine the box is genuinely closed.

When the candle is finally removed, the left thumb pushes in the protruding section while the right hand holds the opposite end of the match-box. As the section is pushed inwards, the 'gimmick' will be forced out into the waiting hand and, once more, is secretly palmed.

At this stage the box can be handed out for examination, and whilst this is being done the other hand, containing the 'gimmick', places the candle to one side, at the same time disposing of the gimmick.

A perfect little illusion for adult shows, but not for children, for obvious reasons.

HOW TIME FLIES

Another new party trick, and an ideal one to introduce when conversation begins to flag.

A small pill-box is displayed and shown to be completely empty. A wrist-watch, without strap, is next shown and can be examined by any spectators who may wish to do so. The performer next asks someone to set the hands of the watch at any time he likes and then to place the watch inside the box and secure the lid in position.

The performer takes the box in his right hand and places it behind his back for a few seconds. He concentrates deeply then reveals the actual time set by the spectator. As an extra climax, the watch may be shown inside the box, finally being secured by the lid held tightly with elastic bands. The performer holds the box in front of him and allows it to fall. The lid, base and elastic bands fall to the table but there is no sign of the watch, which has completely vanished.

The performer remarks 'Time certainly does fly,' as he produces the watch from elsewhere.

PRESENTATION AND WORKING

The requirements are a watch, from which the strap or bracelet has been removed, a pill-box of the type illustrated in the drawing and large enough to hold the watch, and an elastic band. As no special preparation is needed, the trick can be presented impromptu at any time.

When the box has been examined and shown to be empty, the face of the watch is displayed and the hands revolved by the winder to show that any time can be set. It is also shown that the watch fits inside the box, face uppermost, and that the lid fits tightly on top.

The watch is then handed to a spectator who is asked to set a time upon the face, place the watch inside the box, and secure the lid. While this is taking place the performer turns his back on the guests, with hands clasped behind his back, waiting to receive the box containing the watch. After a few moments' concentration, he announces the time set by the spectator.

It is during this stage that the secret working takes place.

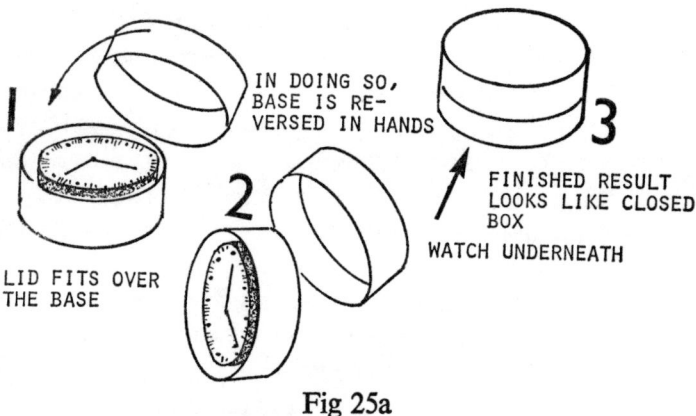

Fig 25a

When the box is placed in the performer's hands, he turns round to face the guests. Behind his back he quickly removes the lid, reverses the box (so that it is upside down) and then replaces the lid now on the top (which is actually the base of the box).

When the box is now displayed before the audience it looks exactly the same as before. It also means that while displayed at an angle, and because the base is open, the watch face is visible to the performer at a glance, so that he can note the time. This should be done smoothly, without obvious peering—a casual glance at the watch face for a moment whilst pattering to the audience will suffice. (See pictures on p 36.)

As the performer recaps on the actions already carried out, he again places the box behind his back so that he can transfer the lid to its correct position. He then announces the correct time-setting and hands the box containing the watch for checking by the member of his audience who originally set the hands.

The trick may be repeated several times if desired, but it is advisable not to overdo it.

A novel climax can be introduced into this trick in which the watch is made to vanish from the box. Place the box containing the watch on your left palm. Then, as the right hand comes over, apparently to put the lid on the box, it provides the necessary cover to make the 'secret' move which the audience must not see. The left hand, in fact, allows the box to pivot over so that the bottom is uppermost. At the same time the right hand quickly places the lid on what is now supposed to be the top position. The audience can hear the watch inside the box as the performer rattles it, and is convinced that it is well and truly in the box. The next move must look as though your right hand removes the box from the left, and this is done quickly. As the box is lifted away, the left hand turns over, retaining the watch in the palm position. The three illustrations on page 36 should make this simple 'move' even clearer to follow.

To the audience, you are simply holding the box containing the watch in your right hand. You then announce that you require an elastic band, which should be in the left-hand pocket of your jacket. Your left hand, (concealing the watch) goes to the pocket for this, leaving the watch behind and bringing out the elastic band. This is placed around the box, keeps lid and base together.

To make the final 'vanish' of the watch, the band is removed slowly and discarded, and the box is allowed to drop to the table, so that the audience suddenly realise that it is now empty. They can then be allowed to examine the box and see that it has not been tampered with. If the performer wishes to reproduce the watch, he has simply to reach into his pocket and display it. If he wants to produce it elsewhere, perhaps in another part of the room, a duplicate will have to be used and previously hidden.

Where only one watch is used, a good tip is to stick an adhesive spot on the glass face of the watch, and get a spectator to initial it, so that when it is reproduced he can confirm that it is the same watch.

Coupling this reproduction with the clever vanish makes an intriguing little mystery, and the illusion has the advantage that all the objects used can be closely examined both before and after the effect.

PERSONALITY DOMINOES

This is a game of dominoes, but with a difference. Instead of the standard spotted set, these 'dominoes' bear the names of your guests. Each half (there are always two sections on a domino) has a different name written or printed upon it. The first may have 'Mary' on one side and 'Tom' on the other, whilst the next will have 'Tom' one side and 'Jane' on the other, and so on.

95

All the 'dominoes' are mixed up and held in one stack by the performer. As they are very thin (stiff cardboard is ideal) they can be handled much like playing-cards.

A guest is asked to select any one, which is then displayed and the guest is asked to remember the names written upon it. It is then replaced amongst the others and another guest is asked to 'cut' the pack of 'dominoes' over and over again, thus losing the chosen one amongst the others. The pack is then handed back to the performer who repeats the cuts, thus making sure that even the spectators do not know the position of the selected 'domino'.

Handing the 'dominoes' to yet another guest, the performer explains that the game will now begin and that the 'dominoes' must be laid out as in a normal game of dominoes. When the guest has completed the chain of 'dominoes' it will be found that the names on each end of the chain are those on the 'domino' originally selected.

THE WORKING AND PRESENTATION

The 'dominoes' used can be made from stout cardboard and should measure approximately 3in by 1½in with a dividing line in the centre. On one section write or print the name of one of your male guests and on the opposite half the name of a female guest. Carry on until the names of all your guests are recorded. It does not really matter how many guests you have at your party; the more the better, and the longer the chain is the more bewildering is the effect of the climax.

Once you have the 'dominoes' made, with a sharp knife cut off a strip at an angle, as shown in the drawing, from one end of each card. Note that it must be a tapered cut. When the stack is held together it tapers slightly but this is not noticeable. When one card is reversed in the stack, the opposite end, being completely straight, protrudes from the tapered cards. Thus you know which card has been reversed. This is the basic secret and working of the trick.

Let us assume that you have displayed the 'dominoes' and spread them out on the table. You now explain that the names of the guests appear on them and that one 'domino' has to be selected. The pack is then carefully gathered together, making sure all tapered ends finish up at one side and fanned towards any guest with the request that he selects one of them. It should be emphasised that he has a perfectly free choice—which, in fact, he has.

When one has been removed, the performer must secretly reverse his pack of 'dominoes' so that when the chosen one

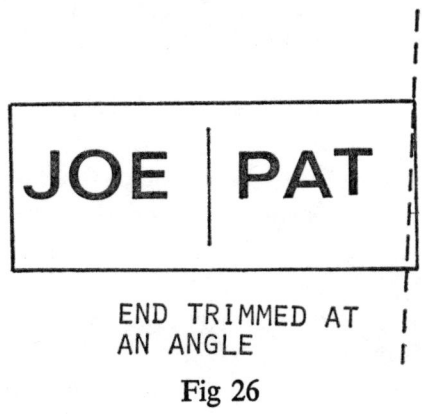

END TRIMMED AT
AN ANGLE

Fig 26

is replaced amongst the others, it will obviously be the only reversed one in the set. A simple method, but an effective one.

With this 'domino' still reversed in the pack, the pack can be handed to any other guest, who is asked to cut it several times, completing each cut. This does not affect the working in any way. When the pack is returned to the performer he can immediately 'strip' (a 'magician's' term given

97

because of the nature of each card) out the selected card by simply feeling for the protruding portion. A pretence is made of cutting the 'dominoes' once or twice, but in reality this chosen one is 'stripped' to the top position. This domino, bearing the names which will complete the chain at each end, is then secretly palmed and dropped into the performer's pocket while the rest are laid on the table. Before the game actually starts, the performer can make his prediction, writing the names upon a piece of paper which is then placed inside an envelope and presented to a spectator.

The game begins and when the chain of 'dominoes' is complete, those on both ends will bear the predicted names.

This is a trick that can never fail and one that may be repeated several times, providing you replace the 'stolen' domino and remove one of the others.

MEMORY BOOK TEST

This is a sophisticated mental mystery which can be presented at any adult party. Television viewers will have seen several performers present just such an experiment using normal books.

Two books are displayed to the guests, who are asked to choose which one shall be used.

The performer will previously have announced that this is a memory test and that he has memorised the first word on every page of both books. When one of the books has been selected, a guest is asked to call out the number of any page from Page 1 to the actual number of pages in the book. Let us say in this instance a 200-page book is used. The performer, concentrating for a few seconds, writes his prediction on paper, or chalks it upon a slate. The guest then calls out the first word on the page he selected and this is found to be the very word which the performer predicted.

THE WORKING AND PRESENTATION

First you must obtain two copies of the same book. Although the books are identical, their dust jackets are not. One belongs to the book, the other you will have borrowed from some other book, but to the audience you will appear to be using two different books.

Now for the subtle working and simple, if rather 'cheeky', method.

A piece of paper, or a school slate and a piece of chalk should be ready to hand for you to write down your prediction.

You display the two hard-backed books, one in each hand, talk about their contents and make the point that they are different. You then ask a guest to select one of the books, making it clear that he may change his mind if he wishes and that whichever book he discards will not be used in the experiment.

The choice made, you then announce that of the several thousands of words in the two books, you have memorised the first word of every page. You ask a guest to choose a page number and to call it out so that the audience know it and he cannot change his mind, or forget the number, during the effect.

During this routine you will have had in your hand the discarded, but duplicate book and in the course of re-capping you casually open the book, as if demonstrating to the audience how the other book was opened at any page desired. In fact, you riffle quickly through the pages, noting the first word on the selected page, and then stop at another page which you show to the audience. If the chosen page number was, for example, 73, you say 'The first word on page 73 in my book is 'tree', meanwhile carefully covering with your hand the real page number of your book. By this diversion, the audience are given the impression that you are simply demonstrating the procedure and re-capping on what has already been done.

You already know the first word on the chosen page and can now discard your book and draw attention to the prediction, which is quickly written or chalked. The guest who selected the page number is then asked to call out the first word on the page and you then display your prediction board to the audience.

It is advisable to have both books in your bookcase among others, so that when you announce the experiment they will appear to have been selected casually.

This impressive little demonstration will probably earn you the reputation for a superman's memory whereas, in fact, its main requirements are a smooth presentation and some acting ability.

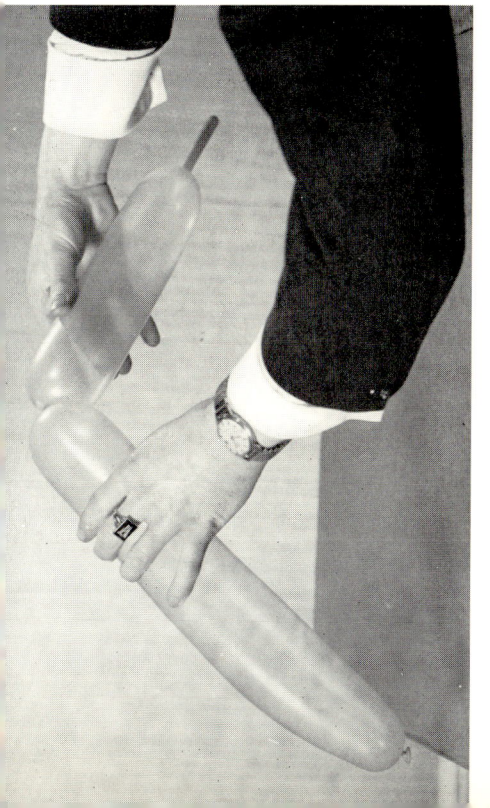

Page 101 : **Balloon Modelling**: (*top left*) a balloon twist; left hand holds balloon firmly while right hand twists balloon in clockwise direction; (*below left*) The Swan; (*above*) The **Poodle**

Page 102: Hand shadows: (*top left*) The basic hand shadow; (*top right*) Man wearing hat; (*bottom*) Sir Winston Churchill

7

Fortune-telling for the Party

FORTUNE-TELLING is an ideal entertainment at most adult parties, and especially where older people are present. Everyone wants to know what the future holds and provided it is not taken too seriously, fortune-telling can offer a pleasant and interesting interlude at any gathering. It is also particularly suitable for outdoor fetes or other functions whose object is to raise funds for some charity or other good cause.

Fortune-telling can be presented in various forms: cards, tea leaves, crystal globes, signatures and horoscopes, and in all cases good 'presentation' is essential if the reading is to be at all convincing.

HOROSCOPES

Many people like hearing about themselves and particular traits in their character, and the following horoscopes are based on commonsense and known facts concerning the signs of the Zodiac. They are not to be taken too seriously, nor are they claimed to be accurate, but they can be relied upon to entertain your party guests and perhaps promote some friendly arguments.

When reading horoscopes, make sure that everyone remains seated and keeps quiet during the procedure. All whose birth-date is in the particular month which is being used should be asked to stand so that the other guests can see to whom the horoscope applies.

A horoscope is given here for each of the twelve months of the year and you can either refer to this book when reading or, better still, type or write a copy so that it will always be readily available to entertain guests at any time.

JANUARY

If you are born in January you have no middle nature; you have power to do great good or great evil and sometimes the evil nature will predominate over the good. In such cases, a hard fight will be necessary to conquer the evil nature and bring the good to the surface. But you can always win the battle if you try, and the victory will be sweeter for the efforts you have made.

Your lucky day—27th.

FEBRUARY

Those born in February are always very sensitive and exacting people; they are quick to take offence but are capable of great tenderness. They go to extremes in their likes and dislikes and are most successful when among those for whom they have affection. When among those whom they dislike, they are apt to get upset and become irritable.

Lucky day—11th.

MARCH

Persons born in this month who marry early in life should

be very careful in their selection of a mate, but if their choice is dictated solely by their heart, their future is sure to be crowned with love and happiness. Persons born this month are easily swayed by others and have little will-power of their own, consequently they should be particularly careful in the selection of their friends.

Lucky day—3rd.

APRIL

Those who are born in this month are kind and affectionate, as well as possessing a great deal of personal magnetism. Very often they succeed as musicians and frequently become great actors and stage stars. They are born under a lucky star and accumulate wealth before middle age. At the sunset of life, these April people are usually endowed with plenty of this world's goods and the ability to enjoy it to the full.

Lucky day—9th.

MAY

People are lucky who have this month for a birthday, and many great men were born in May. Their capacity for love is their weak point; anyone whom they love deeply and sincerely can lead them to do anything, even to commit a crime. Those who are born in May should marry early in life and choose their mate from those born in March.

Lucky day—1st.

JUNE

June people are usually a jolly lot who give no thought for tomorrow, and this is usually their one big mistake in life. They are seldom serious, usually full of fun and take great delight in giving pleasure to others. When in trouble, they feel it deeply at the time but soon get over it, for their happy, sunny nature soon dispels all gloom.

Lucky day—23rd.

JULY

Many people born in this month are apt to have impulsive natures. They want to accomplish things in a hurry, never stop to think about a problem, but dive right in and then wonder why they are not always successful. They are also inclined to attach too much importance to the material things of life.

Lucky day—2nd.

AUGUST

Fortunate indeed is anyone who was born in August. There is no end to what they can achieve, provided they aim at worthwhile objectives. The right choice of friends is important, for they can help a lot. August people are adept with both their brains and their fingers and are at their best when using them both at the same time.

Lucky day—17th.

SEPTEMBER

Many who were born in September possess strong will-power and are at their best when following pursuits that call for the use of their mental faculties. They are great thinkers and prone to reason out their own ideas and methods. They will not take advice from others until it has been proven beyond the shadow of a doubt that their own method is wrong.

Lucky day—1st.

OCTOBER

Persons born in this month are best suited to literary or

artistic pursuits. They have a keen eye for art and often make first-rate critics. They are quick to perceive the good in anything or anybody, and seldom see the bad unless pointed out to them. They are upright and honourable and usually credit other people with being the same.

Lucky day—6th.

NOVEMBER

Those who were born in this month are strong in some things and correspondingly weak in others, so that their lives are apt to be somewhat erratic. They are great home-builders and love everything pertaining to home and its comforts. They should guard against jealousy, which often causes them quite unnecessary unhappiness.

Lucky day—15th.

DECEMBER

Many people born in this month are natural leaders, and some of the type that would make good dictators. They are extremists. When happy they are very happy, but when sad, they are thoroughly miserable. They are loyal, kind-hearted and generous, and while they never forget a kindness, they are 'big' enough to forgive an injury.

December people are usually ones who do many things, but as they are inclined to rush into action without proper planning, their output is apt to be large but the quality only average. They are usually lone wolves, keep secrets to themselves, and often talk in a low voice.

Lucky day—20th

CHARACTER FROM SIGNATURES

Many interesting facts about a person can be deduced from a signature, and as no two are alike a careful study can often result in a shrewd assessment of salient points in the writer's character.

A signature which cannot be read easily may simply mean

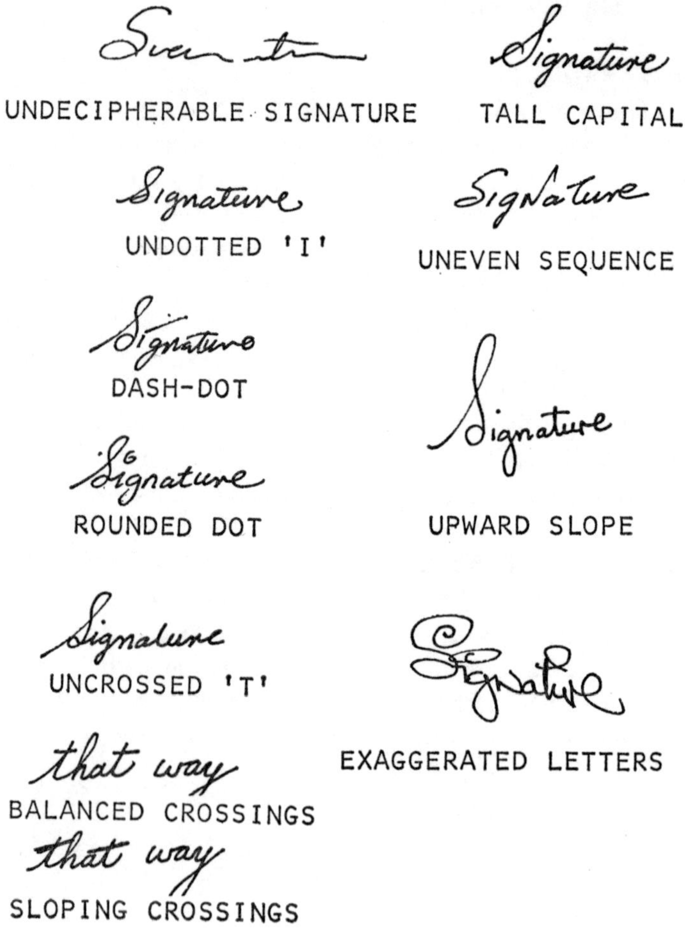

UNDECIPHERABLE SIGNATURE

TALL CAPITAL

UNDOTTED 'I'

UNEVEN SEQUENCE

DASH-DOT

ROUNDED DOT

UPWARD SLOPE

UNCROSSED 'T'

BALANCED CROSSINGS

EXAGGERATED LETTERS

SLOPING CROSSINGS

Fig 27

that the writer is always in a hurry. On the other hand, it can also indicate carelessness and untidiness.

Undotted 'i's' suggest that the writer has a bad memory, whereas if he *does* dot all his 'i's', he is probably careful and a stickler for detail. It is also known that someone who dots the 'i's' is reliable and capable of concentration on subjects in which he or she is interested.

A dash instead of a dot over the 'i's' indicates that the writer is a decisive, perhaps rather aggressive type, but one with a strong sense of humour.

An 'i' dotted in the form of a circle shows that the writer is artistic, or could be giving a false impression. The 'circled' dot often means that the writers had time on their hands in which to go back to the 'i' to make this design. The same applies to the letter 'j'.

When the letters are crossed, such as the letter 't', the writer is usually a careful, if not a cautious person. If the cross has been omitted, it suggests a bad memory and the writer is usually absent-minded. But if each crossing is correctly and uniformly placed, this is the sign of a well-balanced personality. A heavy cross through the letter indicates that the writer, though in a hurry, is still decisive and knows exactly what he is doing.

Capital letters immediately indicate certain characteristics.

A large capital letter at the beginning of a signature shows that the writer is secure, perhaps even over-confident, whilst a sequence of capital letters mingled with smaller ones indicates someone who is indecisive and insecure.

Many people have two signatures, one for personal use, and one for business. If you find a person uses both, he or she can often be trying to impress and is unlikely to be sincere.

Here are some other points to look for when studying signatures.

If the letters tend to slope upwards, the writer is ambitious.

Clear and even letters indicate an honest type of person, while letters which do not conform to standard are a sign that the writer has an original turn of mind and may well be artistic.

Tall letters with long capitals are indicative of personal pride.

Letters which appear to be cramped signify a rather selfish personality.

When the final letter of a signature is rounded, the writer is one who can be generous.

Exaggerated letters, bold and large, are the sign manual of a boastful character.

A downward stroke on letters shows that the writer is distrustful.

Letters which end in a diminished fashion tend to suggest that the writer is insincere.

A person who uses only the essential minimum of strokes is probably of an economical, if not rather stingy turn of mind.

Although it may be hard to believe, the foregoing deductions are really based on commonsense, and though they differ from other readings, they have frequently proved to be accurate.

PALMISTRY

Reading a person's character from their palm can be both interesting and entertaining. Once the 'fortune-teller' has carefully studied the various lines of the palm, as shown in the accompanying drawing, he or she should be able to give a convincing display of character-reading and fortune telling.

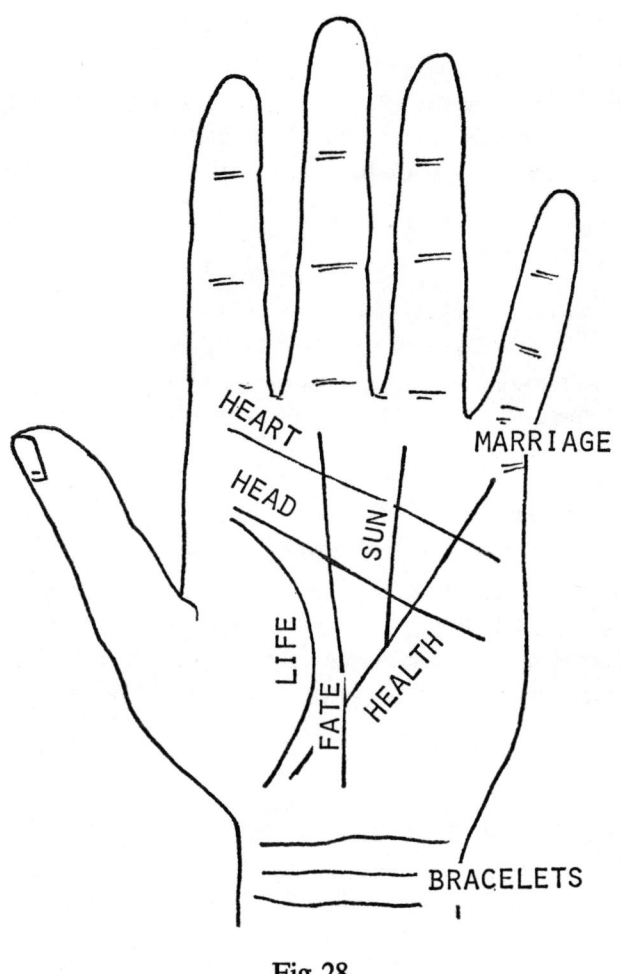

Fig 28

PRINCIPAL LINES

HEAD LINE
This is the line which determines the person's intelligence. If the line should run right across the palm it means that that person can usually carry through major decisions, and can be relied upon for good judgement in most matters.

HEART LINE
If this line should be clearly shown on the palm, it indicates capacity for love and devotion, and certain success in marriage. If it extends from one edge of the palm to the other, it could be a sign of jealousy leading to unhappiness. If the line is not a clear one, selfishness and lack of devotion are indicated.

LIFE LINE
This line determines the life span of the individual. Should it extend to the wrist, the person will have a long life ahead of him and if the line is consistent, he will enjoy a well-balanced life. A broken line may be a sign of difficulties and unforeseen happenings, most of which will be overcome.

SUN LINE
A clear line shows the individual to be accurate and artistic, and if the line be lacking in clarity, the reverse. If the line is a long one, unhappiness lies ahead, mainly because of a lack of confidence in pursuing a goal in life.

FORTUNE-TELLING BY TEA-LEAVES

One of the oldest methods of fortune telling, a 'reading' of tea-leaves calls, frankly, for some exercise of imagination on the part of the reader. The various shapes or patterns formed by the leaves will suggest an association with some event to an imaginative reader and, coupled with his own shrewd assessment of the character or way of life of his 'client', should enable him to make some credible predictions of events likely to occur in the near or distant future.

A wide-mouthed tea cup is to be preferred and it should be white inside and free from decoration. The tea—no tea bags or instant tea!—is poured from the pot into the cup without using a tea-strainer and when most of it has been drunk by the prospective 'client', he or she is asked to quickly tilt away the residue into a saucer or slop basin, leaving a formation of leaves on the base and one side of the cup. The 'reader' then takes over and if, for example, he perceives a shape resembling a heart, 'love' is obviously suggested and can be given a variety of interpretations according to the age and sex of the 'client'. The shape of a bell could suggest

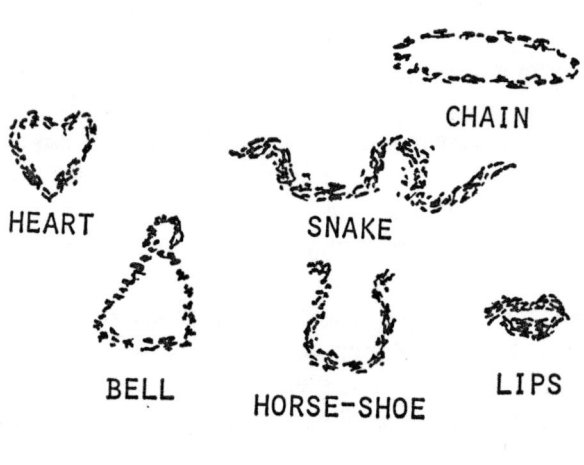

Fig 29

good news, perhaps early tidings of a long-awaited event; anything slightly resembling a horse-shoe could foretell a happy future or a possible coming share of good fortune, while a chain suggests an imminent wedding, which need not necessarily be that of the 'client' but perhaps of some relation. Incidentally, before predicting marriage for one's 'client', it is as well to be sure that he or she is not already married and the partner among the listening guests.

The shape of a snake could be a warning to be on guard against someone plotting mischief and anything in the form of an aeroplane obviously suggests an imminent journey. There are no 'set' designs, but the illustrations in Fig 29 depict some which frequently occur.

FORTUNE-TELLING BY CARDS

'Reading the cards' is one of the most popular of all methods of fortune-telling and can provide excellent entertainment at most adult parties. It is as well, however, to remember, and perhaps to remind one's guests, that it *is* an entertainment and that card readings should never be taken too seriously. It has also often been said that it is unwise to consult the cards more than once a day.

Only thirty-two out of the full pack of fifty-two playing cards are normally used in fortune-telling sessions, all cards from 2 to 6 inclusive being removed from the pack. Each of the thirty-two remaining cards has its own particular meaning and if these can all be memorised, so much the better as one is then prepared for all occasions and a more impressive reading can be given. Alternatively, the cards can be marked with brief inscriptions to serve as an aide-memoire.

PLAYING-CARD MEANINGS

The following are the meanings or significance to be attached to each of the thirty-two cards.

CLUBS
ACE: Often means good luck, unexpected news and good fortune, but if reversed can mean the opposite.

KING: This card means loyalty; someone, usually a stranger, will render you a service.

QUEEN: A dark lady may be there to guide you in trouble. Take her advice; it may be rewarding.

JACK: You may acquire a new and different type of friend. He will be reliable and may be able to put new opportunities in your way.

TEN: Success in many directions, but only if you make full use of your opportunities.

NINE: A gift may come your way. Don't refuse it, for it may change your life for the better.

EIGHT: Romance. A new love may enter your life, one which will bring you happiness.

SEVEN: Good business transactions may become open to you, but only if you are on the alert to recognise them.

HEARTS
ACE: Certainly a love card. A meeting with a new friend may change your life completely. If it leads to love, it could be most sincere.

KING: Your chances in life may be improved if you really believe that you have something to offer society.

QUEEN: A lady looking for good company may be able to help you, not only in your social life but also in business.

JACK: A child may be the answer to your problems. The meeting may be most unexpected but do not underestimate its importance.

TEN: A proposal may come your way, but be careful. Make a point of getting to know the person first before making any final decision.

NINE: A card which enables you to make a wish or even two, but don't be greedy. Think carefully of what you most want in life.

EIGHT: Like the club card, a card of love and romance. In hearts it presages a forthcoming proposal.

SEVEN: Your home comforts have much to offer; a card indicative of a perfect marriage.

DIAMONDS

ACE: Foreshadows a proposal but, if married, unpleasant news.

KING: Be on guard against a dishonest person, for he or she may at first seem to be sincere.

QUEEN: A loyal person wishes to be friendly with you. It could be a colleague whom you work with, or someone living nearby.

JACK: A young man may at first seem interested in you but may later prove a disappointment. For men, it could be a warning against someone who will try to intrude into your life, and who will need to be carefully watched.

TEN: You may be persuaded into undertaking a long journey. Remember that the decision is yours, and consider it carefully.

NINE: There may be disagreements within your family. Be sensible, for such matters are often over-emphasised.

EIGHT: Love is near you, and maybe love in a completely different image.

SEVEN: Arguments are foreseen in the near future. They

may arise from personal or business reasons and could cause trouble if you are not particularly careful.

SPADES

ACE: A card of death. A friend may die soon, or perhaps a pet you have treasured, or have known. But don't take this warning too seriously as it may well be that the worst will not happen.

KING: Money matters should be carefully watched during the next few years, as there may be persons who are out to cheat you.

QUEEN: Take advice from the aged and learn from their experience. But do not ever allow yourself to be dominated by one person.

JACK: You may meet someone in a completely different age group with some new ideas about life in general. Listen but don't take what is said too seriously.

TEN: A card which foretells trouble ahead. It could be either a comparatively minor problem or a serious matter.

NINE: Bad news may come your way, but it could in the end prove to be a blessing in disguise.

EIGHT: You may be disappointed in your work or personal affairs, but this is only a temporary phase and the right moment for you seriously to consider what you really want to make of your future.

SEVEN: Someone you trust may let you down. Do not let it ruin your life for it is the prelude to happier events which are soon to follow.

8

Balloon-Modelling
and Hand-Shadow Entertainment

B ALLOON-MODELLING must surely rank as one of the most original and interesting pastimes yet invented. It enables one to create animals, figures and shapes of all kinds from one or more balloons and can be a most amusing party game not only for children, who will be particularly delighted by it, but also for adults.

Only a few professional entertainers as yet have gained a reputation as balloon modellers but one recalls the famous 'Windy Blow' who toured the music-halls for years and frequently appeared on television. The leading exponent today is Roy Van Dyke, a professional entertainer, who enthralls audiences with the variety of wonderful models he produces with a few simple twists here and there. In the United States, his counterpart is Dwight Damon, well-known on television screens, particularly in the middle West.

Modelling-balloons are available from stores such as Woolworths or from most good toy shops (See Appendix

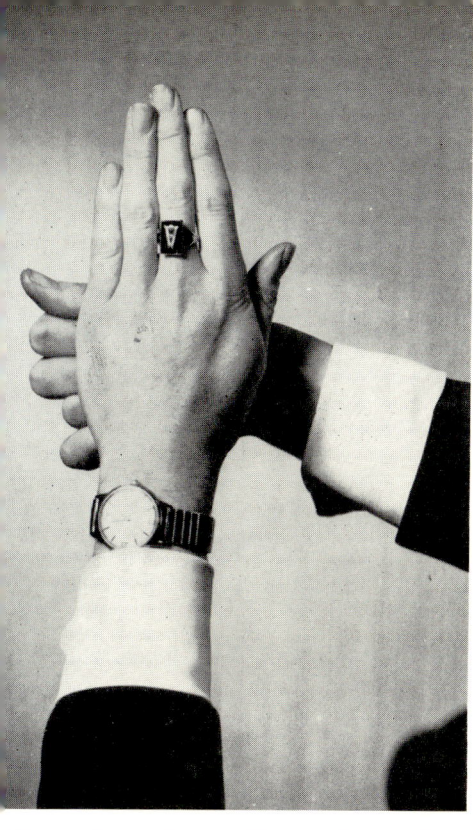

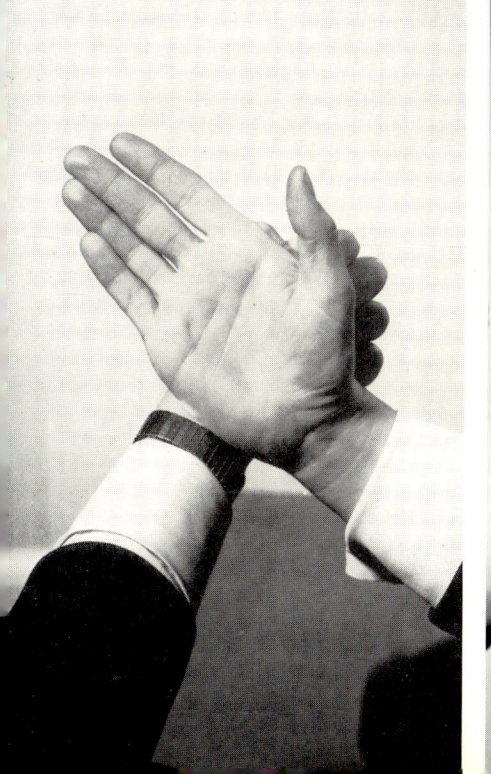

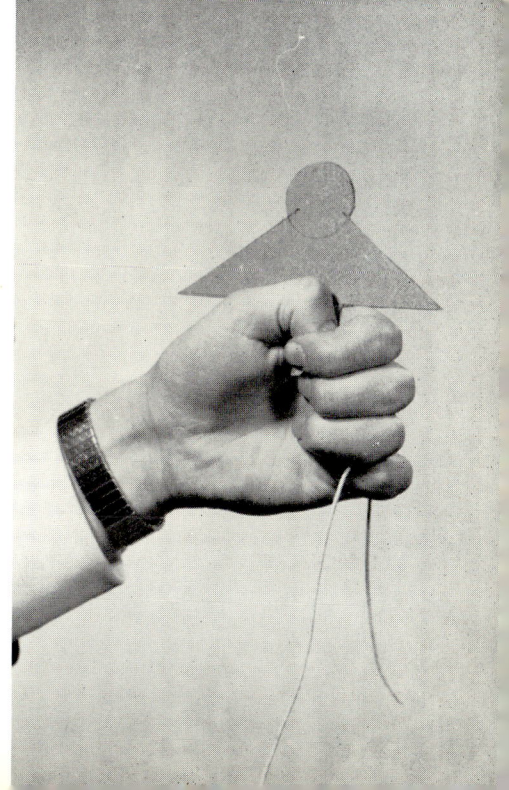

Page 119: Hand shadows: (*top*) The Cowboy; (*bottom left*) The Indian brave; (*bottom right*) The Chinaman

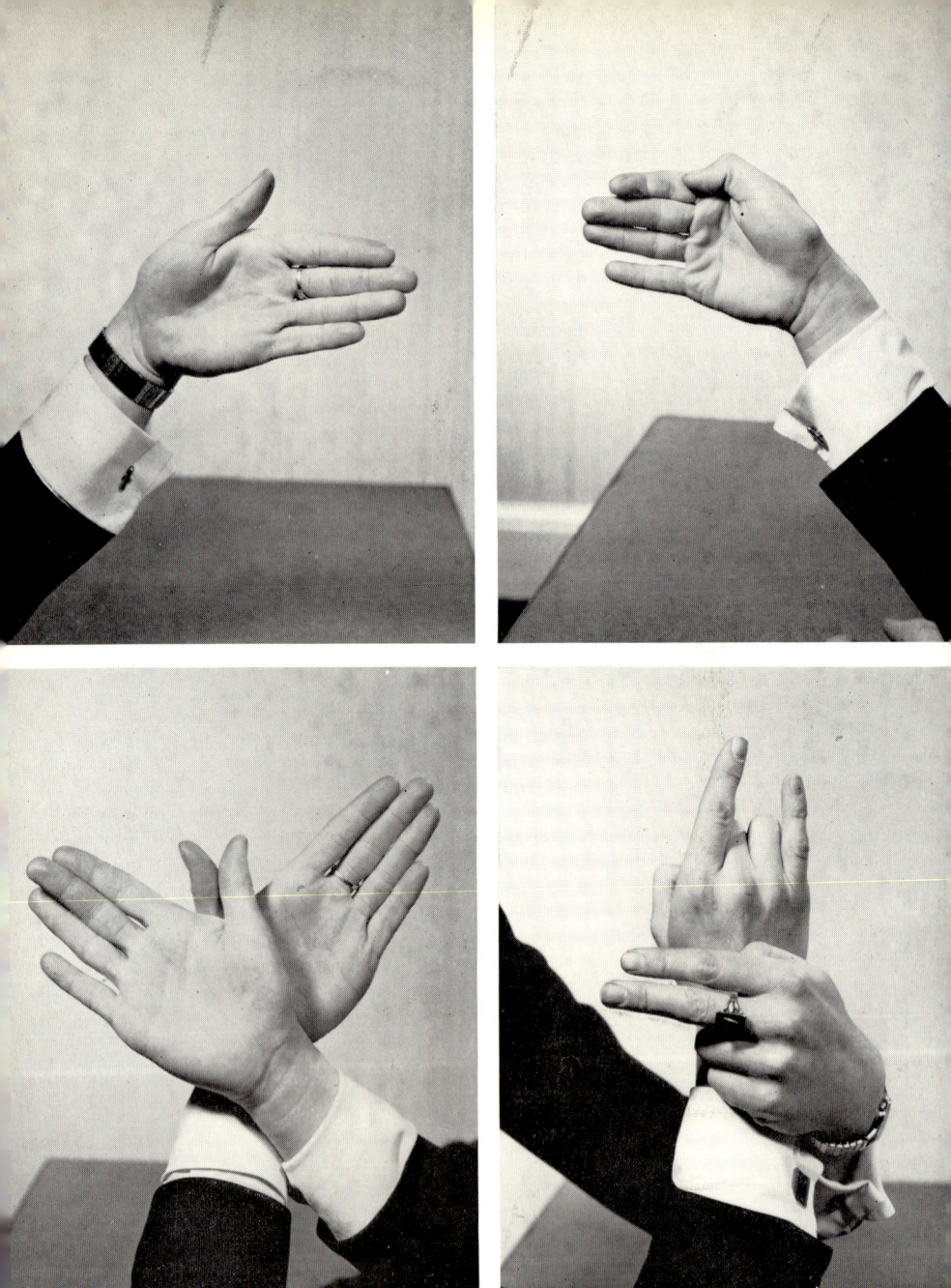

Page 120: Hand Shadows: (*top left*) The Horse; (*top right*) The Wolf; (*bottom left*) The Butterfly; (*bottom right*) The Rabbit

BALLOON-MODELLING & HAND-SHADOW ENTERTAINMENT

for names and addresses of manufacturers). These balloons are so made that they can safely be twisted into various shapes without fear of their bursting, and the finer the quality the better the results. They come in many sizes but four basic types are generally used for modelling. These are numbered 231 (which means 2in wide × 31in long); 340 (3in × 40in); 318 (3in × 18in); and 245 (2in × 45in, USA type). We will refer to them as small, medium, large and extra long, the latter being the best for making an animal or figure from a single balloon.

A balloon inflator, obtainable from the same shops that sell the balloons, can be used to blow up the balloons but is much more fun to inflate them by mouth and this is quite easy when you know the secret. Fill your cheeks with air, put the neck of the balloon to your mouth and *shoot* the air into it. Do not try to fill the balloon in one operation—which is impossible—but expel the air into it gradually until it is partially or completely inflated. When it is full, tie the neck of the balloon by stretching it out lengthwise until there is enough slack for the knot to be tied. Make a tight knot, as if it is loose air will escape and your created model will soon lose shape and collapse.

The secret in twisting a balloon into shape is to do it quickly and slickly. Both ends of the balloon should be held firmly and while the left hand retains the hold, the right twists the balloon in a clockwise direction. (See picture, p 101.) A second inflated balloon can then be twisted around this part, so securing the two in position.

The following drawings show the various 'twists' and 'formations' and these, together with the brief explanations, should enable the reader to build up the models, step by step, without any difficulty.

THE RAT

An easy model to make, this requires only two balloons, one 3 × 40in and another 3 × 18in.

Inflate the long balloon to half its length and tie it tightly.

Inflate the 3 × 18in balloon and twist it half way along its length. Twist the long balloon six inches from the nozzle

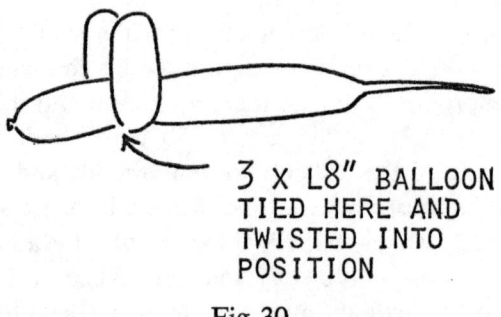

3 X L8" BALLOON
TIED HERE AND
TWISTED INTO
POSITION

Fig 30

end, and then place the 3 × 18in balloon around the twist in the larger one. In doing so, tie the extreme ends of the smaller balloon together.

Now push the twist in the large balloon and the knotted ends of the smaller balloon together.

It is possible to animate the rat, making it move up the arm, by pushing it firmly against the jacket and then releasing it. Hold the end in the left hand, the right hand covering this, and move the model up the arm or jacket front.

THE GIRAFFE

Formed from four balloons, the Giraffe is a fine creation and an excellent example of balloon modelling.

122

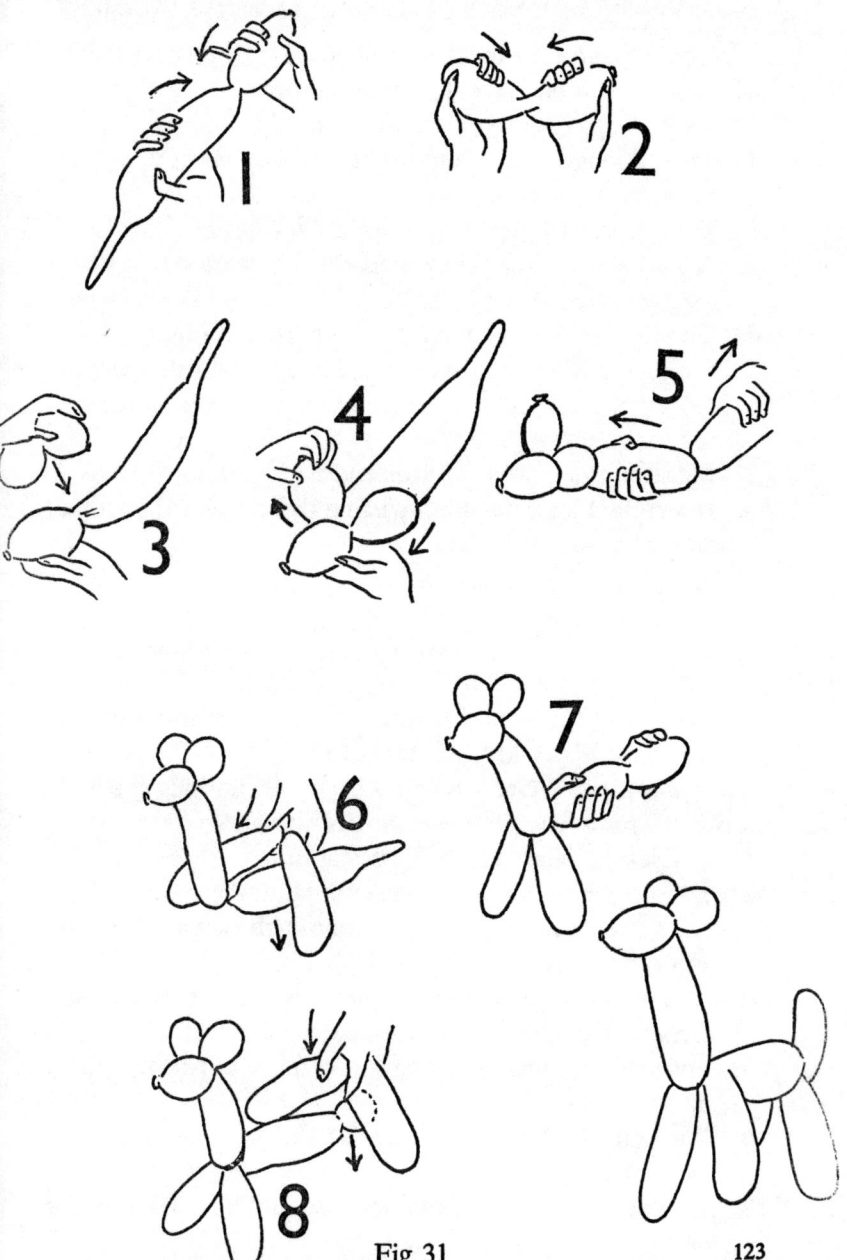

Fig 31

123

Requirements: One short balloon (3 × 18in or similar); Three long balloons (3 × 40in or similar).

Study the following diagrams on p 123.

1 Take a long balloon and make a twist a short way from the end.
2 Twist a short inflated balloon in the centre.
3 Arrow shows how the twisted short balloon crosses with the twist in the long one.
4 The result: note how balloon is twisted around.
5 Make a further twist about half-way down the neck.
6 Now make a twist in the second long balloon and insert. Cross ends to secure.
7 Make another twist towards end for the tail.
8 Insert final long balloon, twisting this in central position, and cross ends to secure.

The end product: the Giraffe.

THE DOG

A neat dog can be made from one balloon, and a perfect model created by adding features to it.

Requirements: One 2 × 45in balloon (extra-long type).

See the following diagrams on page opposite.

1 Balloon is inflated to half its length.
2 Twist it two inches from the end. Hold the twist.
3 Now twist the balloon again one inch down as shown, and then twist the first part in half.
4 Extreme end is twisted around the other twists and tucked through the joint to secure.
5 Twist three inches along and then a further three inches.
6 Turn end under, twist again, as shown, and tie around twist 'A'.
7 To make the head, and ears, use similar twists as for

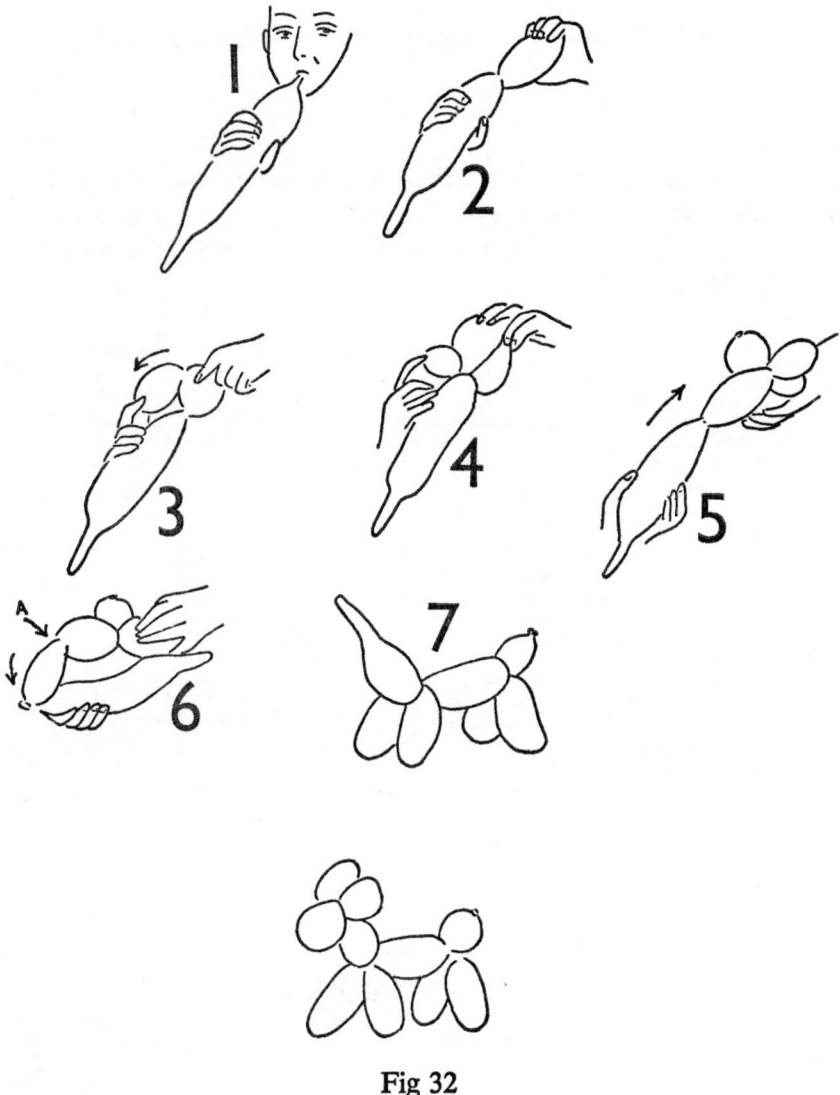

Fig 32

the legs and tail. Finally add features with a 'magic marker' pen or black charcoal crayon.

The last diagram (not numbered) shows the final result.

THE SWAN

In most packets of balloons, white ones are mingled with those in brighter colours. These white balloons are particularly suitable for this model, but of course any colours can be used.

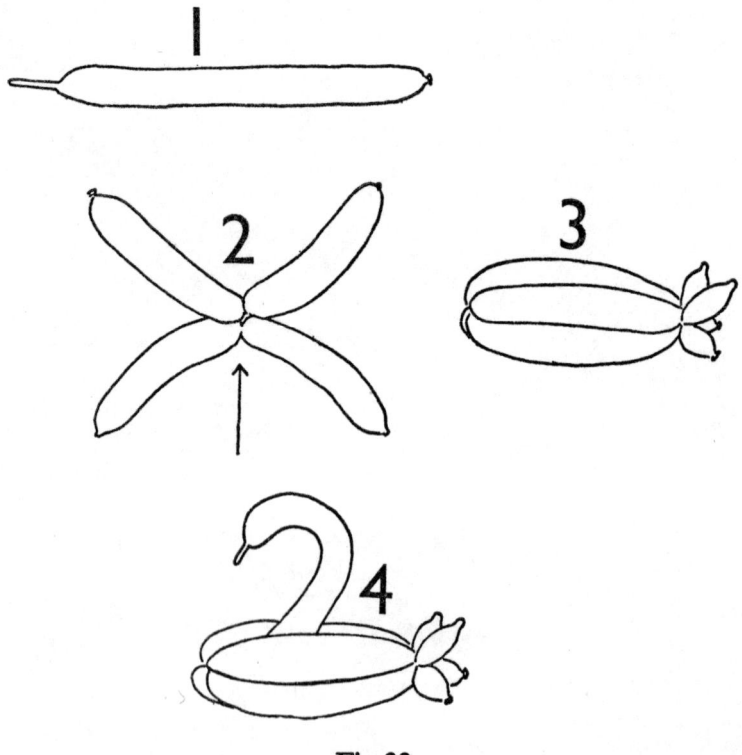

Fig 33

Requirements: Three 2 × 31in balloons are used. First take two of these and inflate them. Hold them firmly in the centre and twist them. Diagram 2 should show this clearly. Gather the four ends of the balloons together, as shown in the next illustration, but make sure you retain hold of these throughout the next moves. When the ends are together, twist these so they appear as a tail. This forms the body of the swan. (Diagram 3.)

Take the final balloon and inflate it so that the end resembles the beak of the swan.

Before inserting it into the others, twist and bend this several times so that it retains a curved appearance; when completed, force it into the body as in Diagram 4.

If wished, your creation can be handed out to one of your guests, particularly if it is someone who is celebrating a birthday or a wedding anniversary. Features can be added to the swan with the aid of a marker pen, but this is not necessary and may spoil the model unless very well done.

The picture on p 101 shows the completed swan.

THE POODLE

The completed model is shown on p 101.

Requirements: One large 340 balloon and three small 318 balloons.

First inflate the 340 balloon to half size and tie it. The three small balloons should be already inflated but their ends should contain enough air so that the tying of the balloons will be made easier.

A small 318 balloon is then tied around the big one about eight inches from the nozzle end. Make a twist in the big balloon at this point and then push the tied ends of the 318 balloon into this twist and secure it in position. The nose and ears of your poodle have now been made.

127

The nozzle end of the big balloon is pushed against the 318. Curl hands around the 318 balloon (ears of the dog) and keep a firm but steady pressure with the thumbs on the big balloon; then push the 318 through to form the head of

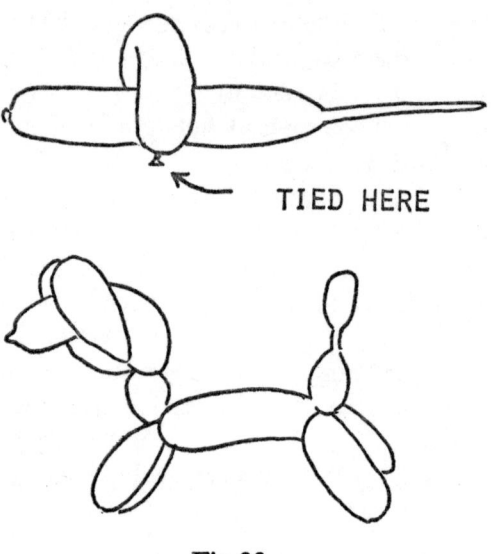

TIED HERE

Fig 33a

the poodle.

Continue to make the rest of the body. Twist the neck into position and insert the second 318 balloon, which has been twisted in the middle, and cross over to secure. Repeat this procedure further along with the third short balloon, forming the hind legs and tail. Make sure there is a bubble of air in the tail as well as a part which is not inflated.

Twist the air bubble in the dog's tail in half and work the air above the twist right up into the inflated part of the tail. Then let the twist unwind and you will find that you have an authentic poodle-type tail.

This model is from the Roy Van Dyke collection.

128

HAND-SHADOW ENTERTAINMENT

The creation of figures, animals and suchlike from the shadows cast by a pair of hands behind a well-lit screen is a well-tried form of entertainment, though less often seen nowadays than it used to be. It makes an excellent interlude for a party and though generally associated with children, adults can also be entertained by the creation of recognisable silhouettes of well-known politicians, film stars and other familiar faces. The show will also be enhanced if accompanied by some carefully rehearsed 'patter' relating to the figure shown on the screen.

THE SCREEN

Though far more elaborate types of screens can and have been used, the following model is one of the simplest, yet perfectly effective for its purpose. As can be seen from the drawing, it consists of a linen blind stretched over a simple wooden frame. Protruding legs allow the frame to stand up-

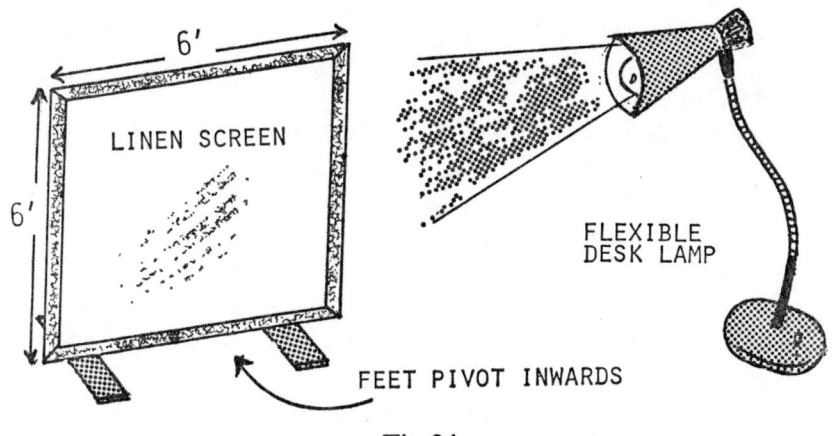

Fig 34

right on a table-top, preferably a card table. The linen blind should be white and stretched as taut as possible over the frame. The entire screen should be about six feet square. Behind the table and screen, there is a chair for the performer.

THE LIGHTING

A simple unit consists of a flexible desk lamp whose beam can be pointed in any direction. Failing this, a normal table lamp could be used and its light directed on to the screen by a dark shade. The lamp is placed on a chair behind the performer, who is half-way between the screen and the lamp, and is so placed that the beam projects over his shoulders onto the screen but does not shine directly into the eyes of the spectators facing the screen.

It is advisable to have an assistant at hand, ready to switch off the normal room lighting when the show is about to start, and whilst the performer will normally be seated when creating shadows with only one hand, it will add to the effect if he stands towards one side of the screen when using both hands so that the audience can see his manipulations.

THE HANDS

Though the hands form the greater part of the shapes projected on the screen, it is not always possible to achieve the required detail with these alone. The face of a cowboy, for instance, could be formed by the hands but his hat would have to be supplied by a cardboard cut-out. Other simple cut-out shapes, such as hats, pipes, handkerchiefs etc, will help to make each figure more effective and more easily recognisable.

Here are brief descriptions of the hand manipulations needed to depict a number of tried and tested designs, all

130

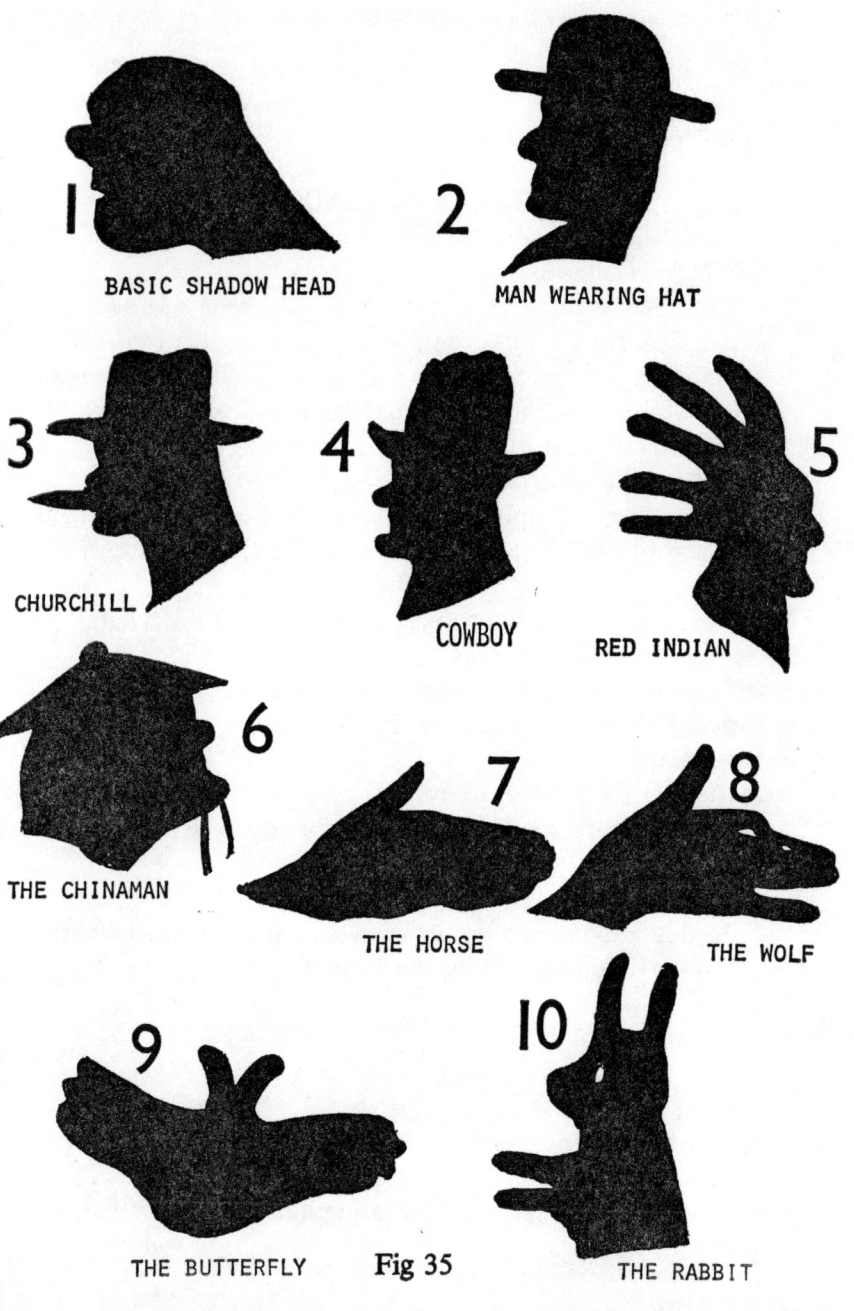

1 BASIC SHADOW HEAD

2 MAN WEARING HAT

3 CHURCHILL

4 COWBOY

5 RED INDIAN

6 THE CHINAMAN

7 THE HORSE

8 THE WOLF

9 THE BUTTERFLY

10 THE RABBIT

Fig 35

lifelike in appearance and easily presented by anyone who follows the instructions and studies the drawings and photographs.

FIGURES IN SHADOW

1 *Basic Head Shadow*

The picture on p 102 shows how the bent fingers and knuckles form the basic outline of a head. Faces can differ by moving the knuckles into various positions, thus giving the 'character' a longer or curved nose. Experiment with this position for it can be used in many ways.

2 *Man wearing Hat*

By adding a simple flat cardboard cut-out hat, inserted between the thumb and forefinger of the first position, the head appears to be wearing a hat.

The picture on p 102 depicts this clearly.

3 *Sir Winston Churchill*

Taking this position one step further, we can present famous characters such as Sir Winston Churchill. The picture on p 102 shows the position, slightly altered, but with the well known 'trilby' upon his head and a cut-out cigar coming from his mouth. The shadow on the screen is excellent.

4 *A Cowboy*

In this instance the hat is formed by the left hand whilst the other hand resembles the head and features. Picture, p 119.

5 *A Red Indian*

Here the right-hand fingers are used to good effect, forming the Indian brave's head-dress. The picture on p 119 shows the correct position.

6 *A Chinaman*

With the aid of a length of string and flat cut-out hat, a

perfect resemblance is achieved. Note the slight difference in the formation of the fingers. Picture, p 119.

7 A Horse

Forming animal silhouettes is just as easy, and the first is so simple that anyone can do it immediately. The hand is simply held outstretched with protruding thumb at the top, forming the ears. Picture, p 120.

8 A Wolf

Same position as the example above, except that the index finger is curled inwards slightly, giving the wolf a rather 'fierce look'. By manipulating the little finger, the wolf can open and close its mouth. Picture, p 120.

9 A Butterfly

Both hands are used together to form this model. By flapping the hands back and forth, the butterfly on the screen will appear alive. Picture, p 120.

10 A Rabbit

Again, both hands are used and the reader will be able to follow the hand positions from the photograph and then study the 'shadow drawing' showing the final result. (Where fingers are extended to form hands or claws, it is possible, of course, for the model to pick up various objects.) Picture, p 120.

9

Outdoor Parties and Fund-raising Events

THOUGH garden parties, in the formal sense, are no longer as popular as they once were, there is much to be said for making full use of one's garden, if only as an adjunct to any indoor entertainment. If the weather is fine, refreshments—tea or a buffet supper—can be served in a hired marquee or in the open air, games for young children can be organised while their parents or older children are being entertained indoors, and when a dance is the order of the day there is no more delightful 'sitting out' place on a warm evening than an attractive garden with chairs or seats tactfully arranged in pairs in quiet corners.

Most outdoor functions, however, on any scale—except perhaps for wedding receptions in private gardens of adequate size—are likely to be held in aid of some charitable or other fund-raising object. These may be staged in the garden of a private house generously made available for the occasion or, more usually, in the playing-field of a local school, a cricket ground (with the pitch carefully enclosed

134

and protected!) or a small paddock. The general methods of organising such a function are much the same as those outlined in an earlier chapter for indoor church parties, inasmuch as the talents, services and help of the local community are enlisted, and one person should be placed in full overall charge of the proceedings.

With a suitable venue freely available, plenty of willing helpers and some imagination on the part of the organisers in devising novel attractions with which to extract money from the visitors, any such outdoor event should involve comparatively little expenditure and be sure of making a useful profit for the charity concerned. The following are a few suggestions as to the various types of stalls that could be set up.

BOTTLE STALLS

The stall is set up with a large variety of bottles of all shapes and sizes containing an equal variety of fillings, beer, shampoo, vinegar, aspirins, perfume, fruit drinks, mineral waters or even plain milk. The bottles may be donated, or at least supplied at reduced cost, by local shopkeepers—a visit to the local public-house will usually produce a variety of bottles, empty or full, according to the generosity of the publican—and others will have been provided and filled by friends and colleagues of the organiser. If necessary, a selection of bottled products can also be purchased to supplement the display.

The bottles are not 'sold' as such but each is numbered on the back with an adhesive label and a duplicate of the number displayed inside a clear container or bag. Customers pay their money, perhaps 5 or 10p a time, and may then dip into the bag and draw out a number. Some will be blanks, in that there is no correspondingly-numbered bottle, but if the number drawn corresponds to one of the bottles on display the customer collects it as his prize.

WHITE ELEPHANT STALLS

This type of stall differs from the usual 'jumble sale' inasmuch as the goods offered for sale are new and attractive and will have been donated by those helping to promote the event. Hand-knitted cardigans, pots of honey, books and magazines presented to the organisation by local traders are but a few of the interesting items which visitors are likely to be willing to buy, knowing that their contributions will help a good cause.

GROCERY STALLS

At most outdoor fund-rasing fetes a grocery stall is always acceptable. Fresh eggs from the farm, home-made jams, in fact, all kinds of dairy produce are likely to be readily bought by people who may not always need them but wish to contribute to the event. The goods offered can be gathered from many sources, and local farmers, grocers and traders generally are usually willing to help.

In addition to the stalls, various types of 'side shows' can be kept going throughout the day and very often such a stand, featuring one particular game or entertainment and manned by one person alone, can rake in as much or even more money than a well-stocked and much larger stall. Here are some suggestions which require little preparation and involve no great expense:

BOTTLE OF MONEY

For this you need a 7lb confectioner's jar—which you

will have to purchase as there is a refund on such jars—
in the screw-on lid of which a slot has to be cut. The jar
is then filled three-quarters full with water, a small tot glass
placed inside on the base of the jar, and the screw-on lid
replaced.

When the stall is 'in business', patrons are invited to try
and drop a coin through the slot into the small tot glass.
This is a lot more difficult than it looks and the majority
of the coins will tend to drift away and land on the base of
the bottle. When the occasional one does land in the small
glass the lucky player is presented with one of the small
prizes displayed on the stand. A useful tip is to put several
coins inside the small glass before the show starts—just to
show that it really can be done!

SURPRISE EXPRESS

The requirements here are: a clockwork engine, a circular
track signposted at intervals with the names of, say, a
dozen different towns, and twelve cards bearing the names
of the twelve towns. Paying customers are invited to select a
card and when all have been sold, or as many as seems likely,
the engine is wound up and launched on to the track. When
it eventually comes to a halt the player holding the card
bearing the name of the nearest town receives a prize, the
balance of the takings going to the charity's fund.

OUTDOOR HOOPLA

A pole is impaled in the ground and at a suitable distance
from it (previously determined by trial and error on the
part of the promoter!) a chalk line is marked behind which
the players must stand. Each paying customer is handed six

wooden or cardboard hoops and receives a prize if he succeeds in getting at least four of the hoops over the pole. If the promoter has done his homework properly few people will manage to get more than one or two hoops over the pole and the fund will benefit accordingly.

BALLS IN THE BUCKET

This is by no means a new game but one which has been successfully used at fairgrounds and fetes for many years.

A row of metal buckets, placed at an angle on a wooden stand, plus a few wooden balls, are the requirements. A player is handed six balls and must get at least three of these into a bucket to win a prize. Several people may play at the same time, thus adding to the fun and keeping the trade going. The game looks easy, but most people will find that the balls will bounce out of the buckets. At fairgrounds, an experienced 'grafter' usually comes out front and, to show how easy it is, throws all the balls into the bucket every time. The secret is simple but the method needs practice. The ball must be thrown towards the back of the bucket, when it will drop inside, whereas most people try to throw the balls inside, intending to hit the base, in which case the balls will invariably bounce out again.

A SLIDE IN A BOTTLE

Another bottle game, and again a large 7lb jar is required. A glasscutter will cut a slot through both sides of the jar for you, and these should be cut towards the top so that a flat plastic or wooden strip can be pushed through and held in position. The slot should be large enough for any coin to pass through.

The aim of the game is for the spectator to roll a coin

through the slot so it will come out at the opposite end. Although the feat may look easy, it is, in fact, extremely difficult and any coins which do run along the strip and drop out are indeed lucky ones. Coins which fall off the strip automatically fall to the base of the jar. Any spectators who are successful in retaining their coin receive a small prize, such as a pencil, a comb, or some similarly priced object.

GUESSING THE WEIGHT

Throughout the day a large cake, probably baked and presented to the organisers by some well-wisher, is displayed upon a china plate. Spectators pay a small fee, lift up the plate and try to guess the weight of the cake. They write their answers, together with their name and address, on slips of paper provided by the promoter and these slips are then placed in a box which will be opened at an advertised time towards the end of the fete. Whoever has correctly guessed the weight of the cake, or come nearest to it, so receives it as his prize.

HOW MANY BEANS?

A large jar containing haricot beans is the centre of attraction on this stand. A card boldly asks *'How many beans are in the jar?'* Spectators pay a small entry fee and write down their guess. At the end of the day the organisers check through the slips, decide which number is nearest the correct figure, and announce the name of the prize-winner over a microphone.

WHEEL OF FORTUNE

The piece of apparatus required for this attraction consists of a wooden wheel, boldly painted in various colours. Upon each coloured section a separate number is displayed, and paying customers obtain duplicates of these in the form of wooden sticks or cards. A central spinning arrow with a bold pointer is spun around fairly quickly and spectators eagerly wait for this to stop at one of the numbers. A prize is presented to the person who holds the corresponding number. Town names, playing-cards, solid colours, or pictures cut from advertisements can all be used to good advantage, but numbers are probably the most effective and less liable to confusion.

PICK A STRAW

This is another game well-known through the fairground business and one that can be relied upon to raise money at very small cost.

A panel is set up on the stand displaying a number of photographs or pictures. These can be pictures of film stars, pop singers, politicians or simply of animals, flowers or common objects cut from newspapers or magazines. Nearby is a glass jar or tumbler containing a number of drinking straws into each of which a slip of paper has been previously inserted. Most of the slips are blank but some carry the names of the picture on display. The slips can easily be removed with the aid of a thin rod and the holder of any slip bearing a name is a prizewinner.

OTHER FUND-RAISING ATTRACTIONS

A surprising number of other attractions will often be found to be available, even in a small town or village, if the organisers are enterprising enough, and once it is known that a charity or other good cause will benefit from the occasion.

140

Some local resident with an interesting hobby might, for example, be willing to stage a display, such as a collection of model locomotives, stamps, butterflies or even paintings, for which a small viewing fee could be charged. Scottish dancing, or folk dancing, is always a popular attraction and if there is a local society it might well be pleased to put on a show that would help to attract visitors to the fete. Judo exhibitions, archery contests, and pony rides around the grounds are yet other attractions which might be introduced, while stalls serving tea, coffee, mineral waters and ice cream can be relied upon for patronage and as a source of additional revenue.

INSURANCE SAFEGUARDS

The one major snag about outdoor events, whether they be private parties or charitable, fund-raising events is, of course, the vagaries of the weather and the larger and more elaborate the party the greater the risk of disappointment or even downright disaster.

There is nothing one can do to ensure a fine day for one's party but one can insure against bad weather, at least to the extent that the organisers will be spared any financial loss if the day is a 'washout'. Such insurances, known as 'Pluvius' policies, can be taken out to cover all kinds of outdoor events, from personal holidays to garden parties, fetes, sports meetings and the like, and any insurance company or broker will quote a premium for a specific event. The premium will be based on a number of factors: the coverage required, the geographical location of the venue (some parts of the country are notoriously wetter than others) and the duration of the policy, and payment of the insurance benefit will usually be dependent upon a stated minimum of rainfall, measured in inches, during the period covered by the

141

policy. In most cases the premiums required are far from unreasonable and certainly the organisers of any large-scale outdoor event involving advance expenditure would be very well advised to take out, or at least to obtain a quotation for, a policy of this nature.

In addition to bad weather, there are other risks to which organisers of outside events may be subjected and against which they would be most unwise not to have insured themselves. For example:

1 Fire insurance cover for marquees, tents, stalls and their contents.
2 If casual labour is employed, cover should be arranged to insure against those legal liabilities that rest upon the organisers under the Employers' Liability Acts.
3 There would be legal liability for any accidents or injuries to members of the public or damage to their property due to negligence on the part of the organisers. Insurance protection against any such claim could be arranged under a public liability policy and the limit for indemnity for any one occurence should not be less than £100,000.
4 If large sums of money were likely to be involved, it would be advisable to arrange theft cover against any loss that might be incurred. Similarly, if valuable cups or trophies were to be presented, suitable 'all risk insurance' should be arranged.

All in all then, a visit to the local insurance broker would obviously be a wise precaution for anyone planning an outdoor event of any importance. 'It will never happen to us' may be something to hope for, but if it does, the resultant disaster can only be attributable to bad organisation and lack of foresight.

APPENDIX

Recommended Reading and Manufacturers and Suppliers of Materials Suitable for Party Entertainments

BOOKS

Conjuring as a Craft, Ian Adair (David & Charles)
The ideal book for the host or hostess wishing to entertain his or her friends. The secrets of conjuring are entertainingly explained stage by stage, so that the reader can build up a genuine skill, or just enjoy learning how the tricks are done. Many items suitable for the party atmosphere are explained in this 160-page book which is fully illustrated with line drawings and action photographs.

How to be a Conjuror, Robert Harbin (Sphere paperback)
A paperback edition of Robert Harbin's popular *How to be a Wizard,* this is a complete guide to magic for the beginner. Television magician Harbin offers his readers magical effects which are suitable for all to build and perform. Household items such as match-boxes, paper, string, cards—all articles which would not be out of place at parties—are used throughout the experiments. Containing 175 pages of expert advice, this is an ideal book for anyone wishing to add some 'magic' to the party fun.

Parties and Entertaining, Myra Street (Collins)
Specially devoted to party entertaining, this book contains some 95 large, 8in × 10 in pages, with full colour photographs and illustrations. It covers simple recipes for sophisticated parties, as well as special catering for the children. Seasonable events are tackled and the foods which are suitable for them. A reasonably priced book for the host or hostess looking for novel presentations of food for social occasions.

Origami (The Art of Paper Folding), Robert Harbin, (Teach Yourself Books)
Robert Harbin is the leading authority on Origami, a pleasing pastime most suitable for party entertainment. In this book, with the aid of fine illustrations, the reader is shown, step by step, how to create the most intricate shapes imaginable of animals, figures and suchlike. The standard Origami code is used, so that the beginner as well as the more advanced exponent will be able to follow the instructions without difficulty.

Cocktails (How to Mix Them), Robert, (Herbert Jenkins)
This neat pocket-book of some 112 pages deals admirably with the subject of cocktail mixing. From the varied selection given, the reader will find many types suitable for his or her parties. These range from non-alcoholic cocktails to frappés and from flips to smashes.

MANUFACTURERS AND SUPPLIERS
OF PARTY ACCESSORIES

It is not always possible to obtain specialised party supplies in one's home town, and where difficulty is experienced the following list of suppliers may be found useful.

ORIGAMI PAPER
Butterfly brand and others are obtainable from most good stationers. They can also be obtained in packets from the following:

The Art Department, Foyle's Book Shop, Charing Cross Road, London WC2.

L. Oppenheimer, The Origami Centre, 71 West Eleventh Street, New York 2, NY USA.

John Maxfield Ltd, (Manufacturers of Origami Papers) 8 The Broadway, Mill Hill, London NW7.

MODELLING BALLOONS
Sold in packets of assorted sizes or by the gross in individual sizes.

The Supreme Magic Company, 64 High Street, Bideford, Devon, England.

D. Glover (Wholesale) Ltd, 203 Scholes Lane, Cleckheaton, Yorks.

CARNIVAL AND PARTY SUPPLIES
Decorations, party hats, crackers, blowouts, streamers, lanterns, masks, wigs, table stationery, flags and pennants, film and television productions.

Beck's British Novelties, 139 Upper Street, London N1.

Barnum's Carnival Novelties Ltd, 67 Hammersmith Road, London W14.

Novelties Wholesale, 11 Christmas Steps, Bristol.

CONJURING APPARATUS
The Supreme Magic Company, 64 High Street, Bideford, Devon.

L. Tannen & Co, 1540 Broadway, New York, NY 10036, USA.

CONJURING AND CHILDREN'S ENTERTAINMENTS
The Secretary, The Magic Circle, 34 Eton Avenue, London NW3.

16MM MOBILE FILM OPERATORS
Bristol: Radioscope Film Service, Tel: 0272-22307.

Coventry: Watso Films Ltd, Tel: 0203-20427.

Denton (Manchester): Mobile Cinema Service, Tel: 061-336-3385.

Dublin: Cavalsons Ltd, Tel: 144841.

Glasgow: 20th Century Movies, Tel: 041-946-1988.

Greenford: Rank Film Library, Tel: 01-997-6666.

Leicester: Bob Sarson Ltd, Tel: 0533-20708.

London: Sound Services Ltd, Tel: 01-542-1096.

Surbiton (Surrey): Ron Harris Cinema Services Ltd, Tel: 01-399-6527.

Wales: Eric Sharp's Entertainments Ltd, Tel: Pontyclum 443.

The major oil companies—Shell, BP, etc—also hire out colour films on golf and other sports. For details, contact their local office.

Acknowledgements

I would like to thank the following authorities in their respective fields for helpful advice and co-operation afforded me in the preparation of this work.

W. J. Barry for his advice on insurance coverage for out-door events.

Roy Van Dyke for permission to describe his personal method of balloon-modelling.

Robert Harbin and Frances Marshall for most helpful information about Origami.

Eric Sharp for background information on mobile film units and their methods of operation.

Decca Record Co and Phonographic Performance Ltd for interesting and practical information on the subject of copyright in relation to records.

Index

Page numbers in bold type denote illustrations